Longman School
Shakespeare

D0241106

Macbeth

John O'Connor, Volume Editor
Beth Wood, Activity Writer
Margaret Graham, Consultant

John O'Connor, Editor
Dr Stewart Eames, Textual Consultant

PEARSON
Longman

Pearson Education Limited
Edinburgh Gate
Harlow
Essex
CM20 2JE
England
and Associated Companies throughout the World

ISBN-10: 0-582-84873-3
ISBN-13: 978-0-582-84873-3

Printed in China
SWTC/03

First published 2004
Third impression 2005

The Publisher's Policy is to use paper manufactured from sustainable forests.

We are grateful to the following for permission to reproduce copyright photographs:

ArenaPAL pages 9 top, 9 bottom right, 63 top; Donald Cooper pages 2, 5, 8, 9 bottom left, 10 bottom, 11 top, 12 top, 13, 14, 15 top, 38, 39 bottom, 62, 76, 77 top, 90, 91 bottom, 126, 127 bottom, 148 bottom, 149 bottom, 182 top, 183 bottom, 197, 216, 217 bottom, 221, 227; Zoe Dominic pages 10 top, 11 bottom, 127 top, 148 top, 149 top, 182 bottom, 217 top; Getty Images page 223; Kobal Collection page 225; Ronald Grant Archive pages 15 bottom, 196; Royal Shakespeare Company pages 12 bottom (Reg Wilson), 39 top (Joe Cocks Studio), 91 top (Reg Wilson), 183 top (Joe Cocks Studio), 218 (Joe Cocks Studio), 219 (Malcolm Davies); Robbie Jack pages 3, 63 bottom, 77 bottom.

Cover photograph: Robbie Jack

Picture researcher: Louise Edgeworth

CONTENTS

ACT 1: SCENE BY SCENE

1 Three Witches plan to meet Macbeth.

2 King Duncan learns that rebels and invaders have been defeated. Macbeth is praised for his bravery in battle, and Duncan names him Thane of Cawdor.

3 The three Witches appear to Macbeth and Banquo. They tell Macbeth that he will become Thane of Cawdor and King of Scotland. They also tell Banquo that his sons will be Kings. After this Macbeth hears that he has been made Thane of Cawdor and he begins to imagine that he can become King.

4 King Duncan names his son Malcolm heir to the throne. Macbeth sees this as an obstacle to his ambition.

5 Lady Macbeth reads a letter from Macbeth telling her what the Witches have predicted. She decides to persuade Macbeth to kill Duncan so that he can become King. Macbeth arrives and tells her that Duncan will be staying at their castle.

6 King Duncan and Banquo arrive at Macbeth's castle. They are greeted by Lady Macbeth.

7 Macbeth debates whether he should kill Duncan. Lady Macbeth persuades him to.

ACT 2: SCENE BY SCENE

1 Macbeth sees a vision of a bloodstained dagger. It seems to be guiding him to kill King Duncan.

2 Macbeth has killed the King. He is so shaken that he has forgotten to leave the bloody daggers near Duncan's attendants so they will be blamed for the murder. Lady Macbeth takes control and returns the daggers to the room.

3 Macduff and Lennox arrive. Macduff discovers the King is dead. Macbeth admits to killing Duncan's attendants because he was so angry that they had murdered the King. Duncan's sons, Malcolm and Donalbain, escape fearing that they will be killed too.

4 Macduff reports the belief that the attendants killed Duncan on the orders of his two sons. Macbeth is to be crowned King.

ACT 3: SCENE BY SCENE

1 Banquo suspects that Macbeth killed Duncan. Macbeth plans to have Banquo and his son Fleance murdered.

2 Macbeth is troubled and anxious. He hints to Lady Macbeth that something is going to happen, but doesn't tell her of his plans to kill Banquo.

3 The murderers kill Banquo, but his son Fleance escapes.

4 Macbeth sees Banquo's ghost at a banquet. He is clearly terrified. He decides to visit the Witches.

5 The Witch goddess, Hecate, is angry with the Witches for leaving her out of their dealings with Macbeth. She promises that Macbeth's confidence in what the Witches show him will be used to destroy him.

6 Lennox and another lord talk about the murders and their suspicions of Macbeth's guilt. They have news that Macduff is with Malcolm in England, planning to return with an army to defeat Macbeth.

ACT 4: SCENE BY SCENE

1 Macbeth visits the Witches again. Their magic apparitions tell him to beware of Macduff, but also that he cannot be killed by a man born of a woman and that he is safe until Birnam Wood marches against him. Macbeth hears from Lennox that Macduff has fled to England.

2 Lady Macduff and her children are murdered on Macbeth's orders.

3 In England, with English help, Malcolm and Macduff plan to get their revenge on Macbeth. Scotland must be freed from the suffering he has caused.

Act 5: SCENE BY SCENE

1 Lady Macbeth is seen sleepwalking, trying to wash blood from her hands. Her actions suggest that her mind is tormented by what she has done.

2 A number of Scottish lords march to join forces with Malcolm and his English army near Birnam Wood.

3 Macbeth hears that Malcolm's troops are coming to get him. He is unafraid because of his confidence in the Witches' predictions.

4 At Birnam Wood Malcolm's soldiers cut branches from the trees to disguise their numbers as they approach Macbeth's castle.

5 Macbeth hears that Lady Macbeth is dead. He is then told that Birnam Wood seems to be moving. Desperate, he decides to lead his soldiers out and fight to the end.

6 Malcolm's army, led by Siward and his son, gets ready to attack.

7 Macbeth kills young Siward, but troops enter his castle. Macduff hunts for Macbeth.

8 Finding Macbeth, Macduff reveals that he was not born of a woman, but by a Caesarean. Macbeth, knowing that this is the end, still fights desperately. Macduff kills him.

9 Macduff enters with Macbeth's head on a pole. All declare their support for Malcolm, the new King of Scotland.

THE ROYAL HOUSE OF SCOTLAND

DUNCAN
King of Scotland
He is murdered by
Macbeth.

MALCOLM
Duncan's elder son
He flees to England
after Duncan is
murdered. He becomes
King of Scotland after
Macbeth.

DONALBAIN
Duncan's younger son
He flees to Ireland
after Duncan is
murdered.

MACBETH'S HOUSEHOLD

MACBETH
Thane of Glamis
He is a general in Duncan's
army and related to
Duncan. He becomes
Thane of Cawdor, then
King of Scotland.

LADY MACBETH
Wife of Macbeth
She helps Macbeth to plan
Duncan's murder and later
commits suicide.

PORTER
*Gatekeeper at
Macbeth's castle*
A comic, drunken figure.

DOCTOR
*In Macbeth's
castle*

SEYTON
*Macbeth's armour
bearer*

GENTLEWOMAN
*Lady Macbeth's
servant*

MURDERERS
*Killers of Banquo, Lady
Macduff and her son*

MACDUFF'S HOUSEHOLD

MACDUFF
Thane of Fife
He is suspicious of
Macbeth and flees to
England. He gets
revenge for the
murder of his family by
killing Macbeth.

LADY MACDUFF
Wife of Macduff
She is murdered at
Macbeth's orders.

SON OF MACDUFF
A boy also murdered at
Macbeth's orders.

Banquo's household

Banquo
*General in King Duncan's
army and a friend of
Macbeth*
He is murdered at
Macbeth's orders.

Fleance
Banquo's son
He escapes the murderers
sent to kill him by Macbeth.

Other Thanes and their households

Ross
He serves Macbeth but
later deserts him. He
informs Macduff of his
wife's murder.

Lennox
He serves Macbeth but later
switches sides to fight
against him.

Angus

Caithness

Menteith

The Supernatural World

Three Witches
They prophesy the future
for Macbeth who comes to
rely on them for their
powers.

Hecate
The Witch Goddess
She is accompanied by
three more Witches.

The English

Siward
*The Earl of
Northumberland*
He is commander of
Malcolm's English army.

Young Siward
Siward's son
He is killed by
Macbeth in battle.

English Doctor
*At the court of King
Edward the Confessor*

RSC, 1982

Queen's Theatre, 1999

West Yorkshire Playhouse, 1999

RSC, 1993

National Theatre, 1972

Albery Theatre, 2002

Teatre Romea / Barbican, 2003

RSC, 1993

Schiller Theatre Company, 1992

RSC, 1986

Battersea Arts Centre, 2000

Shakespeare's Globe, 2001

Shakespeare's Globe, 2001

Tricycle Theatre, 1995

RSC, 1993

Macbeth, 1997 (directed by J. Freeston)

THE SUPERNATURAL WORLD

Three WITCHES

HECATE *the Witch goddess (with three more Witches)*

APPARITIONS

THE ROYAL HOUSE OF SCOTLAND

DUNCAN *King of Scotland*

MALCOLM *his elder son*

DONALBAIN *his younger son*

THE MACBETHS' HOUSEHOLD

MACBETH *Thane of Glamis*

LADY MACBETH *his wife*

a PORTER

a DOCTOR

SEYTON *Macbeth's armourer*

Lady Macbeth's GENTLEWOMAN

OTHER THANES (LORDS) AND THEIR HOUSEHOLDS

BANQUO *a general in Duncan's army*

FLEANCE *his son*

MACDUFF *Thane of Fife*

LADY MACDUFF *his wife*

their young **SON**

LENNOX

ROSS

MENTEITH } *other Scottish noblemen*

ANGUS

CAITHNESS

THE ENGLISH

SIWARD *Earl of Northumberland*

YOUNG SIWARD *his son*

a **DOCTOR** *in King Edward's court*

OTHERS

a **CAPTAIN** *in Duncan's army*

MURDERERS

an **OLD MAN**

LORDS, ATTENDANTS, SERVANTS, MESSENGERS, SOLDIERS

Scenes are set in Scotland, apart from Act 4 Scene 3, which takes place in England, at the court of King Edward.

In this scene ...

- The three Witches plan to meet Macbeth on the heath, as he returns from battle.

3 **hurlyburly**: confusion, i.e. the battle

5 **ere**: before

6 **heath**: open moorland

8–9 **Greymalkin ... Paddock**: names for a cat and a toad, animal shapes taken by the Witches' attendant spirits

10 **Anon**: We're coming at once

Think about

- In the Roman Polanski film, the Witches are shown burying a severed hand during this scene. If you were the director, what would you have them do?

- The Witches declare that 'Fair is foul, and foul is fair' (line 11). What kind of atmosphere is conjured up in this scene? As you read on, think about the ways in which other things seem to be turned upside-down in this play.

Scotland: open wasteland.

Thunder and lightning. Enter three WITCHES.

WITCH 1	When shall we three meet again,
	In thunder, lightning or in rain?
WITCH 2	When the hurlyburly's done,
	When the battle's lost and won.
WITCH 3	That will be ere the set of sun.
WITCH 1	Where the place?
WITCH 2	Upon the heath.
WITCH 3	There to meet with Macbeth.
WITCH 1	I come, Greymalkin!
WITCH 2	Paddock calls.
WITCH 3	Anon!
ALL	Fair is foul, and foul is fair! –
	Hover through the fog and filthy air.

5

10

Exeunt.

toad   pad

Act 1   Scene 2

In this scene ...

- A soldier reports to King Duncan that the rebel Macdonwald and his Norwegian supporters have been defeated.
- He tells Duncan that the Scottish generals, Macbeth and Banquo, performed bravely in the battle.
- Duncan announces that he will sentence the rebel Thane of Cawdor to death and that Macbeth will be given his title.

King Duncan asks for a report of the battle between his forces and a rebel army. A wounded soldier tells Duncan that Macbeth has killed the rebel Macdonwald.

2   **As ... plight**: judging by the bad state he's in

2–3   **revolt ... state**: latest developments in the rebellion

4   **hardy**: brave

5   **'Gainst my captivity**: to save me from being captured

6   **broil**: conflict

7   **Doubtful**: In the balance

8   **spent**: exhausted

9   **choke ... art**: block each other's efforts

10   **for to that**: i.e. to make him a rebel

11   **multiplying ... nature**: evil qualities

12–13   **from ... supplied**: is being helped by soldiers on foot and horse from Ireland and the Hebrides

14   **Fortune ... smiling**: the goddess of luck, favouring Macdonwald in his sinful cause

15   **Showed ... whore**: appeared like a prostitute, following the rebels

17   **Disdaining**: caring nothing for / scorning
      brandished steel: i.e. his drawn sword

19   **Valour's minion**: the special favourite of Courage

22   **unseamed ... chops**: tore him open from the stomach to the jaws

25–6   **whence ... break**: i.e. when fine spring weather often brings storms

Think about

- What sort of imagery does the Captain use? Think about how he conveys the ideas that (a) the battle was in the balance; (b) Macdonwald was wicked; and (c) luck, or fortune, is always changing sides.

Near Forres.

Drums beat a call to arms. Enter DUNCAN, *King of Scotland,*

with MALCOLM, DONALBAIN, LENNOX, *and soldiers.*

Enter (meeting them) a CAPTAIN, *bleeding from his wounds.*

DUNCAN   What bloody man is that? He can report,
                 As seemeth by his plight, of the revolt
                 The newest state.

MALCOLM   This is the sergeant
                 Who, like a good and hardy soldier, fought
                 'Gainst my captivity – Hail, brave friend!   5
                 Say to the King the knowledge of the broil
                 As thou didst leave it.

CAPTAIN   Doubtful it stood –
                 As two spent swimmers, that do cling together
                 And choke their art. The merciless Macdonwald
                 (Worthy to be a rebel, for to that   10
                 The multiplying villainies of nature   villaines slechterik
                 Do swarm upon him) from the Western Isles
                 Of kerns and gallowglasses is supplied –
                 And Fortune, on his damnèd quarrel smiling,
                 Showed like a rebel's whore. But all's too weak –   15
                 For brave Macbeth (well he deserves that name),
                 Disdaining Fortune, with his brandished steel
                 Which smoked with bloody execution,
                 Like Valour's minion, carved out his passage
                 Till he faced the slave –   20
                 Which ne'er shook hands, nor bade farewell to him,
                 Till he unseamed him from the nave to the chops,
                 And fixed his head upon our battlements.

DUNCAN   O valiant cousin! Worthy gentleman!

CAPTAIN   As whence the sun 'gins his reflection,   25
                 Shipwrecking storms and direful thunders break –
                 So from that spring, whence comfort seemed to come,

The soldier describes how
Macbeth and Banquo then
fought off an attack by the
rebels' supporters, the invading
Norwegians. Ross and Angus
arrive with a further report of
the battle.

30 **skipping**: lightly armed
    trust their heels: i.e. run away
31 **surveying vantage**: seeing his opportunity
32 **furbished arms**: fresh weapons

35 **As ... lion**: i.e. Macbeth and Banquo
    were no more frightened than fierce
    creatures would be of timid ones
36 **sooth**: truth
37 **over-charged ... cracks**: with double
    charges of gunpowder
39 **Except**: Unless
    reeking: i.e. steaming
40 **memorise another Golgotha**: make the
    battlefield as memorable as the scene of
    Christ's crucifixion
44 **smack**: are a sign

45 **Thane**: Scottish lord

46 **What ... eyes**: By the look of him, he's
    in a great hurry

50–1 **flout ... cold**: i.e. fly insultingly and put
      cold fear into our people
54 **dismal**: ominous (i.e. it looked as
    though it would end badly for the
    King's army)
55 **Bellona's ... proof**: Macbeth, heavily
    armoured, as though newly married to
    the goddess of war
56 **self-comparisons**: i.e. comparable skill
    and courage

Think about

• What do we know about
Macbeth so far? Think about
how his physical courage
and his capacity for
violence are described.

Discomfort swells. Mark, King of Scotland, mark!
No sooner justice had, with valour armed,
Compelled these skipping kerns to trust their heels,   30
But the Norwegian lord, surveying vantage,
With furbished arms, and new supplies of men,
Began a fresh assault.

DUNCAN   Dismayed not this
Our captains, Macbeth and Banquo?

CAPTAIN   Yes –
As sparrows eagles, or the hare the lion!   35
If I say sooth, I must report they were
As cannons over-charged with double cracks –
So they doubly redoubled strokes upon the foe.
Except they meant to bathe in reeking wounds,
Or memorise another Golgotha,   40
I cannot tell –
But I am faint. My gashes cry for help.

DUNCAN   So well thy words become thee, as thy wounds:
They smack of honour both. – Go, get him surgeons.

Exit CAPTAIN, *helped by soldiers.*

Enter ROSS *and* ANGUS.

Who comes here?

MALCOLM   The worthy Thane of Ross.   45

LENNOX   What a haste looks through his eyes!
So should he look that seems to speak things strange.

ROSS   God save the King!

DUNCAN   Whence cam'st thou, worthy thane?

ROSS   From Fife, great King –
Where the Norwegian banners flout the sky   50
And fan our people cold.
Norway himself, with terrible numbers,
Assisted by that most disloyal traitor,
The Thane of Cawdor, began a dismal conflict –
Till that Bellona's bridegroom, lapped in proof,   55
Confronted him with self-comparisons,

Ross reports that Macbeth has defeated the Norwegians. King Duncan orders that the rebel Thane of Cawdor shall be put to death and his title given to Macbeth.

58 **Curbing ... spirit**: i.e. disciplining Cawdor for daring to oppose the King

62 **craves composition**: is begging to discuss peace terms
63 **deign**: allow / grant
64 **disbursèd**: paid
    Inch: island

67 **our bosom interest**: matters close to our heart
    present: immediate

---Think about---

- Who was who in the battle that has just taken place? Name (a) the rebel Macbeth killed; (b) Macbeth's fellow general in the King's army; and (c) the Scottish traitor who assisted the Norwegians.

- What line from Act 1 Scene 1 does Duncan's final statement (line 70) remind you of? What is the effect of that echo?

Point against point, rebellious arm 'gainst arm,
Curbing his lavish spirit. And, to conclude,
The victory fell on us –

DUNCAN   Great happiness!   **60**

ROSS   – That now
Sweno, the Norways' king, craves composition.
Nor would we deign him burial of his men
Till he disbursèd at Saint Colm's Inch
Ten thousand dollars to our general use.   **65**

DUNCAN   No more that Thane of Cawdor shall deceive
Our bosom interest! – Go, pronounce his present death,
And with his former title greet Macbeth.

ROSS   I'll see it done.

DUNCAN   What he hath lost, noble Macbeth hath won.   **70**

Exeunt.

In this scene ...

- Returning from the battle, Macbeth and Banquo meet the three Witches.
- They tell Macbeth that he will be Thane of Cawdor and King, and Banquo that he will be father to a line of kings, though never King himself.
- After the Witches have vanished, Ross and Angus arrive to tell Macbeth that he has been given the title Thane of Cawdor.
- Although Banquo warns him that Witches try to lure people to evil, Macbeth is excited by their prophecies.

The first Witch describes how she is going to torment a sailor whose wife has been rude to her.

2 **swine**: pigs

6 **quoth**: said
7 **Aroint thee**: Get out of here
   rump-fed ronyon: over-fed hag
9 **But … sail**: People believed that witches could sail in sieves.
11 **I'll do**: i.e. I'll do him mischief

15 **have all the other**: i.e. have power over all the other winds
17–18 **quarters … card**: compass-points on a sailor's chart

21 **penthouse lid**: eyelid
22 **forbid**: under a curse

24 **dwindle … pine**: i.e. grow thinner and waste away
25 **bark**: ship

Think about

- What does the Witches' proposed spell against the sailor tell us about how they might treat Macbeth?

- How would you describe the rhythm and rhyme scheme of the Witch's curse (lines 15 to 26)? How does it fit what she is saying?

A heath.

Thunder.

Enter three WITCHES.

WITCH 1	Where hast thou been, sister?
WITCH 2	Killing swine.
WITCH 3	Sister, where thou?

WITCH 1   A sailor's wife had chestnuts in her lap,
And munched, and munched, and munched.   5
'Give me,' quoth I.
'Aroint thee, witch!' the rump-fed ronyon cries.
Her husband's to Aleppo gone, master o' the *Tiger* –
But in a sieve I'll thither sail,
And like a rat without a tail,   10
I'll do, I'll do, and I'll do!

WITCH 2	I'll give thee a wind.
WITCH 1	Th' art kind.
WITCH 3	And I another.

WITCH 1   I myself have all the other –   15
And the very ports they blow,
All the quarters that they know
I' the shipman's card.
I'll drain him dry as hay!
Sleep shall neither night nor day   20
Hang upon his penthouse lid;
He shall live a man forbid.
Weary sev'n-nights nine times nine,
Shall he dwindle, peak and pine.
Though his bark cannot be lost,   25
Yet it shall be tempest-tossed!
Look what I have.

WITCH 2   Show me, show me.

Macbeth and Banquo see the Witches who greet Macbeth, addressing him as Thane of Glamis, Thane of Cawdor and King. Banquo asks them who they are.

29   pilot: sailor / navigator

33   weird sisters: sisters who share in the powers of fate, i.e. the Witches
34   Posters: fast travellers
36   Thrice: three times

38   wound up: completed

40   is't called: is it supposed to be

41   attire: clothing

43   aught: the kind of creatures

45   choppy: chapped / with cracked skin

Think about

• What can we tell from Banquo's speech (lines 52 to 58) about Macbeth's initial reaction to the Witches' prophecies?

• What do you think the Witches' 'charm' (line 38) may be intended to do?

51   hereafter: at some time in the future

54   fantastical: imaginary
56   present grace: his current title (i.e. Thane of Glamis)
57   Of noble ... hope: i.e. as a man who will achieve even greater fortune and the chance of being King
58   rapt withal: completely carried away / in a trance

WITCH 1   Here I have a pilot's thumb,
                Wrecked, as homeward he did come.   30

Drum beats in the distance.

WITCH 3   A drum! A drum!
                Macbeth doth come.

ALL   The weird sisters, hand in hand,
                Posters of the sea and land,
                Thus do go about, about –   35
                Thrice to thine, and thrice to mine,
                And thrice again, to make up nine.
                Peace! – the charm's wound up.

Enter MACBETH *and* BANQUO.

MACBETH   So foul and fair a day I have not seen.

BANQUO   How far is't called to Forres? –
                (*seeing the* WITCHES) What are these,   40
                So withered and so wild in their attire? –
                That look not like th' inhabitants o' the earth
                And yet are on't? – Live you? Or are you aught
                That man may question? You seem to understand me,
                By each at once her choppy finger laying   45
                Upon her skinny lips. You should be women,
                And yet your beards forbid me to interpret
                That you are so.

MACBETH   Speak, if you can! – What are you?

WITCH 1   All hail, Macbeth! Hail to thee, Thane of Glamis!

WITCH 2   All hail, Macbeth! Hail to thee, Thane of Cawdor!   50

WITCH 3   All hail, Macbeth – that shalt be King hereafter!

BANQUO   Good sir, why do you start and seem to fear
                Things that do sound so fair? (*To the* WITCHES) I' the
                    name of truth,
                Are ye fantastical, or that indeed
                Which outwardly ye show? My noble partner   55
                You greet with present grace, and great prediction
                Of noble having and of royal hope,
                That he seems rapt withal. To me you speak not.

Banquo asks the Witches to predict his future. They tell him that his descendants will be kings, though he himself will not. Macbeth tries to question the Witches, but they vanish.

59 look ... time: i.e. predict the future

68 get: be the father of
     be none: will not be one

71 imperfect: unfinished, i.e. they tell only part of the story
72 Sinel: Macbeth's father
74 prosperous: successful and wealthy
75–6 Stands not ... more: is no more believable

78 blasted: windswept
79 charge: order

Think about

• What do you notice about the different ways in which the Witches greet Macbeth and Banquo? How might we account for the difference?

• How could the Witches 'vanish' (line 79) in a performance? Think how they might be made to vanish in: (a) a school hall; (b) a modern theatre; (c) Shakespeare's Globe; and (d) a film.

82 corporal: flesh and blood
83 Would: I wish

85–6 the insane ... prisoner: hemlock, or similar plant, which drives people mad

	If you can look into the seeds of time,	
	And say which grain will grow, and which will not,	**60**
	Speak then to me, who neither beg nor fear	
	Your favours nor your hate.	

WITCH 1   Hail!

WITCH 2   Hail!

WITCH 3   Hail!   **65**

WITCH 1   Lesser than Macbeth, and greater.

WITCH 2   Not so happy, yet much happier.

WITCH 3   Thou shalt get kings, though thou be none.
So all hail, Macbeth and Banquo!

WITCH 1   Banquo and Macbeth, all hail!   **70**

MACBETH   Stay, you imperfect speakers! Tell me more.
By Sinel's death, I know I am Thane of Glamis –
But how of Cawdor? The Thane of Cawdor lives,
A prosperous gentleman – and to be King
Stands not within the prospect of belief   **75**
No more than to be Cawdor. Say, from whence
You owe this strange intelligence? Or why
Upon this blasted heath you stop our way
With such prophetic greeting? Speak, I charge you!

                                        The WITCHES *vanish.*

BANQUO   The earth hath bubbles, as the water has,   **80**
And these are of them. – Whither are they vanished?

MACBETH   Into the air – and what seemed corporal, melted
As breath into the wind. – Would they had stayed!

BANQUO   Were such things here, as we do speak about?
– Or have we eaten on the insane root   **85**
That takes the reason prisoner?

MACBETH   Your children shall be kings.

BANQUO   *You* shall be King.

MACBETH   And Thane of Cawdor too – went it not so?

Ross and Angus arrive to give Macbeth some news. As a reward for having defeated the rebels, King Duncan is giving him the title Thane of Cawdor. Angus explains that the existing Thane of Cawdor was a traitor and is due to be executed.

92 **venture**: daring

93–4 **His wonders ... his**: i.e. he does not know whether to praise you or express his amazement

96 **stout**: brave

97 **Nothing afeard**: completely unafraid

99 **post with post**: one messenger after another

103 **herald ... sight:** lead you to his presence

105 **for an earnest**: as a promise

107 **addition**: title

Think about

- What does the news that Ross brings (lines 90 to 108) show about Duncan's opinion of Macbeth? What effect do you think it might have on Macbeth at this point, bearing in mind the Witches' prophecies?

- Look at Macbeth's aside (lines 117 to 118). What is going through his head that he is not willing to share with the others?

110 **Who *was***: The man who used to be
     yet: still

112 **combined**: allied, i.e. fighting on the same side as

113 **line**: strengthen

114 **vantage**: advantages

115 **wreck**: ruin

116 **capital**: carrying the death penalty

118 **behind**: yet to come

BANQUO	To the selfsame tune and words. Who's here?	

Enter ROSS *and* ANGUS.

ROSS	The King hath happily received, Macbeth,	90
	The news of thy success. And, when he reads	
	Thy personal venture in the rebels' fight,	
	His wonders and his praises do contend,	
	Which should be thine, or his. Silenced with that,	
	In viewing o'er the rest o' the selfsame day,	95
	He finds thee in the stout Norwegian ranks,	
	Nothing afeard of what thyself didst make,	
	Strange images of death. As thick as hail	
	Ran post with post – and every one did bear	
	Thy praises in his kingdom's great defence,	100
	And poured them down before him.	

ANGUS	We are sent	
	To give thee, from our royal master, thanks –	
	Only to herald thee into his sight,	
	Not pay thee.	

ROSS	And, for an earnest of a greater honour,	105
	He bade me, from him, call thee Thane of Cawdor:	
	In which addition, hail, most worthy thane! –	
	For it is thine.	

BANQUO	What! Can the devil speak true?	

MACBETH	The Thane of Cawdor lives. Why do you dress me	
	In borrowed robes?	

ANGUS	Who *was* the thane lives yet –	110
	But under heavy judgement bears that life	
	Which he deserves to lose. Whether he was combined	
	With those of Norway, or did line the rebel	
	With hidden help and vantage, or that with both	
	He laboured in his country's wreck, I know not.	115
	But treasons capital, confessed and proved,	
	Have overthrown him.	

MACBETH	(*Aside*) Glamis, and Thane of Cawdor!	
	The greatest is behind. (*To* ROSS *and* ANGUS) Thanks	
	for your pains.	

Macbeth is amazed that the Witches' prediction has come true. Banquo warns him that the Witches might be leading him to evil, but Macbeth begins to think about murdering King Duncan.

121–2 That ... crown: If you believed that, it might encourage your hopes of becoming King

124 win ... harm: lead us to destruction

125 instruments of darkness: agents of evil

126 honest trifles: unimportant truths

127 deepest consequence: things that really matter

129 happy prologues: promising introductions
swelling: impressive / ascending

130 imperial theme: story or topic of being a king

131 soliciting: temptation

133 earnest: promise

136 unfix my hair: make my hair stand on end

137 seated: i.e. fixed in place

140 but fantastical: only in my imagination

141 Shakes ... man: disturbs my being

141–2 function ... surmise: imagination and doubt make me incapable of action

143 rapt: lost in thought / in a trance

145 Without my stir: without my doing anything

146 our ... mould: new clothes, which do not fit properly

147–8 Come ... day: Whatever will happen, will happen, as nothing stops the passage of time

---

Think about

- What does the language of lines 128 to 143 tell us about Macbeth's state of mind?

- What do the following lines have in common: 66, 67, 68, 82, 85 to 86, 132, and 142 to 143? How do they add to the feeling that the natural order of things seems turned upside-down in this play?

                (*To* BANQUO) Do you not hope your children shall be
                    kings,
                When those that gave the Thane of Cawdor to me   120
                Promised no less to them?

BANQUO   That, trusted home,
                Might yet enkindle you unto the crown
                Besides the Thane of Cawdor. But 'tis strange –
                And oftentimes, to win us to our harm,
                The instruments of darkness tell us truths,   125
                Win us with honest trifles, to betray 's
                In deepest consequence. –
                (*To* ROSS *and* ANGUS) Cousins, a word, I pray you.

MACBETH   (*Aside*) Two truths are told
                As happy prologues to the swelling act
                Of the imperial theme. (*To* ROSS *and* ANGUS) I thank
                    you, gentlemen.   130
                (*Aside*) This supernatural soliciting
                Cannot be ill – cannot be good. If ill,
                Why hath it given me earnest of success,
                Commencing in a truth? I am Thane of Cawdor.
                If good, why do I yield to that suggestion   135
                Whose horrid image doth unfix my hair,
                And make my seated heart knock at my ribs
                Against the use of nature? Present fears
                Are less than horrible imaginings.
                My thought, whose murder yet is but fantastical,   140
                Shakes so my single state of man, that function
                Is smothered in surmise, and nothing is
                But what is not.

BANQUO   (*To* ROSS *and* ANGUS) Look how our partner's rapt.

MACBETH   (*Aside*) If chance will have me king, why, chance
                    may crown me,
                Without my stir.

BANQUO   New honours come upon him   145
                Like our strange garments – cleave not to their mould
                But with the aid of use.

MACBETH   (*Aside*) Come what come may,
                Time and the hour runs through the roughest day.

Macbeth hides his thoughts and they all depart to meet King Duncan.

149 **stay … leisure**: are ready to leave when it suits you
150 **favour**: pardon
150–1 **wrought … forgotten**: troubled by past events
151–3 **your pains … them**: i.e. every day I am reminded of what you have done for me
154 **chanced**: happened
155 **The interim … it**: after we have thought it over in the meantime

---
Think about

• What is your impression of Banquo so far? Think about, for example, what his comment to Macbeth (lines 121 to 127) suggests about him, and his attitude to the Witches (line 108).

BANQUO	Worthy Macbeth, we stay upon your leisure.
MACBETH	Give me your favour. My dull brain was wrought 150
	With things forgotten. Kind gentlemen, your pains
	Are registered where every day I turn
	The leaf to read them. – Let us toward the king. –
	(*To* BANQUO) Think upon what hath chanced – and at
	more time,
	The interim having weighed it, let us speak 155
	Our free hearts each to other.
BANQUO	Very gladly.
MACBETH	Till then, enough. – Come, friends.

                                               Exeunt.

Ludlow Festival, 2001

RSC, 1982

RSC, 1976

RSC, 1996

In this scene ...

- Duncan thanks Macbeth and Banquo for the part they played in defeating the rebels.
- Macbeth's secret hope to become King receives a setback when Duncan announces that his eldest son, Malcolm, will be the heir to the throne.

King Duncan's son, Malcolm, reports that the rebel Thane of Cawdor faced his execution with dignity. Duncan thanks Macbeth and Banquo for the parts they played in the battle. Macbeth expresses his loyalty to Duncan.

Think about

- A situation in which the audience knows something important that a character does not is described as 'dramatic irony'. Looking at lines 11 to 14, think about the dramatic irony in (a) the comment being made by Duncan at the very moment Macbeth enters; and (b) the term used by Duncan to greet Macbeth.

---

2   **in commission**: who were given the responsibility (of executing Cawdor)
liege: lord / sovereign

6   **set forth**: displayed

8   **Became ... it**: showed his good qualities as much as the way he died

9   **been ... death**: practised his preparation for death

10   **owed**: owned

11   **As ... trifle**: as though it were something of no value
art: skill

12   **the mind's construction**: i.e. what someone thinks and feels

15   **sin ... ingratitude**: Duncan feels that he has done wrong in not yet rewarding Macbeth.

16–18   **Thou ... thee**: i.e. Macbeth has performed so well that Duncan cannot keep up with the rewards he owes him

18   **Would**: I wish

19–20   **That ... mine**: so that I would have been able to reward you as much as your merits deserve

21   **More is thy due**: you are owed more

23   **pays itself**: is its own reward

26   **but**: only

26–7   **doing ... toward**: protecting

Forres: the palace.

Trumpet fanfare. Enter King DUNCAN, *with* MALCOLM,

DONALBAIN, LENNOX, *and attendants.*

DUNCAN   Is execution done on Cawdor? Or not
            Those in commission yet returned?

MALCOLM   My liege,
            They are not yet come back. But I have spoke
            With one that saw him die: who did report
            That very frankly he confessed his treasons,   5
            Implored your Highness' pardon, and set forth
            A deep repentance. Nothing in his life
            Became him like the leaving it. He died
            As one that had been studied in his death,
            To throw away the dearest thing he owed   10
            As 'twere a careless trifle.

DUNCAN   There's no art
            To find the mind's construction in the face
            He was a gentleman on whom I built
            An absolute trust –

Enter MACBETH, BANQUO, ROSS, *and* ANGUS.

            (*To* MACBETH) O worthiest cousin!
            The sin of my ingratitude even now   15
            Was heavy on me. Thou art so far before,
            That swiftest wing of recompense is slow
            To overtake thee. Would thou hadst less deserved,
            That the proportion both of thanks and payment
            Might have been mine! Only I have left to say,   20
            More is thy due than more than all can pay.

MACBETH   The service and the loyalty I owe,
            In doing it, pays itself. Your Highness' part
            Is to receive our duties. And our duties
            Are to your throne and state, children and servants – 25
            Which do but what they should, by doing everything
            Safe toward your love and honour.

Macbeth is unsettled when
Duncan announces that his
eldest son, Malcolm, will
succeed him as King. Malcolm
is an obstacle to Macbeth's
ambitions, which will have to
be overcome.

31 **enfold**: embrace

33–5 **My plenteous ... sorrow**: i.e. I am so
overcome with joy that I am weeping

36 **nearest**: closest in line to the throne
37–8 **establish ... eldest**: settle who will
succeed to the throne by naming our
eldest son
39 **Prince of Cumberland**: the title held
by the heir to the Scottish throne
39–40 **which ... only**: i.e. the title for
Malcolm will not be the only honour
handed out
41–2 **signs ... deservers**: everybody who
deserves an honour will receive one
43 **bind us further**: increase our debt /
bond us
44 **The rest ... you**: Anything not done on
your behalf is hard work
harbinger: officer sent ahead to make
arrangements

52 **The eye ... hand**: Let my eyes not see
what my hand is doing

Think about

• What does Macbeth's aside
(lines 48 to 53) suggest
about the way his mind is
working at this point? Think
about what he means by
'o'erleap' and what his
'black and deep desires'
might be.

• What image is used in lines
28 to 33? What does
Banquo's reply (lines 32 to
33) suggest about a king's
relationship to his subjects?

DUNCAN	Welcome hither!
	I have begun to plant thee, and will labour
	To make thee full of growing. – Noble Banquo,
	That hast no less deserved, nor must be known **30**
	No less to have done so – let me enfold thee,
	And hold thee to my heart.

BANQUO   There if I grow,
        The harvest is your own.

DUNCAN   My plenteous joys,
        Wanton in fulness, seek to hide themselves
        In drops of sorrow. – Sons, kinsmen, thanes,   **35**
        And you whose places are the nearest, know:
        We will establish our estate upon
        Our eldest, Malcolm; whom we name hereafter
        The Prince of Cumberland – which honour must
        Not unaccompanied invest him only,   **40**
        But signs of nobleness, like stars, shall shine
        On all deservers. – (*To* MACBETH) From hence to
            Inverness,
        And bind us further to you.

MACBETH The rest is labour, which is not used for you.
        I'll be myself the harbinger, and make joyful   **45**
        The hearing of my wife with your approach. –
        So, humbly take my leave.

DUNCAN   My worthy Cawdor!

MACBETH (*Aside*) The Prince of Cumberland! – That is a step
        On which I must fall down, or else o'erleap,
        For in my way it lies. Stars, hide your fires!   **50**
        Let not light see my black and deep desires! –
        The eye wink at the hand! – Yet let that be,
        Which the eye fears, when it is done, to see.

                                                Exit.

Duncan leads his lords away, still praising Macbeth.

54 **full so**: so very

55 **in ... fed**: it is food to me to hear him praised

58 **peerless**: without a rival (i.e. there is no-one to compare with him)

Think about

- In your opinion, what kind of king does Duncan appear to be from these early scenes? Think about how he treats his followers and what they seem to think of him.

DUNCAN   True, worthy Banquo: he is full so valiant,
                And in his commendations I am fed –   55
                It is a banquet to me. Let's after him,
                Whose care is gone before to bid us welcome.
                It is a peerless kinsman.

                                        Trumpets sound. Exeunt.

ACT 1 SCENE 5

In this scene ...

- Lady Macbeth receives a letter from her husband in which he tells her about his meeting with the Witches.
- She fears that he is too good-natured to kill Duncan, and decides to use all her powers to persuade him.
- Receiving news that Duncan plans to spend that night at their castle, she calls upon evil spirits to toughen her for the murder.
- Lady Macbeth advises Macbeth to leave everything to her.

Lady Macbeth reads a letter from Macbeth telling her about the Witches' prophecy that he is Thane of Cawdor and will be King. She worries that her husband has too much natural goodness in him to kill Duncan.

Think about

- What do we learn about Macbeth from his letter to his wife? Has he ever talked to his wife about becoming King, do you think? Has he already decided to kill Duncan? What is his attitude to the Witches?

- What does Lady Macbeth fear about her husband's character? Do you think that fear is justified, from what you have seen so far?

2 **perfectest**: most reliable

5 **rapt ... wonder**: lost in amazement
6 **missives**: messengers

8–9 **coming on of time**: future
10 **deliver thee**: report to you

11 **dues of rejoicing**: i.e. excitement of knowing what great things are in store for you
16 **milk ... kindness**: natural human goodness
17 **catch ... way**: take the quickest route
wouldst: would like to
19 **illness**: wickedness / ruthlessness
attend: accompany
19–20 **What ... holily**: i.e. Anything you really want, you want to get by fair means
20 **wouldst ... false**: you don't want to cheat
21 **wouldst ... win**: you are happy to win unfairly
21–4 **Thou'dst ... undone**: i.e. While you want the murder done, you're afraid to do it yourself
24 **Hie thee hither**: Hurry here
25 **That I ... ear**: So that I can influence you with courage and ruthlessness
26–7 **chastise ... round**: beat down with my arguments everything that stands between you and the crown
28 **metaphysical aid**: supernatural help
29 **tidings**: news

46

Inverness: inside Macbeth's castle.

Enter LADY MACBETH, *with a letter.*

LADY MACBETH (*Reading*) 'They met me in the day of success – and I
have learned by the perfectest report, they have more in
them than mortal knowledge. When I burned in desire to
question them further, they made themselves air, into
which they vanished. Whiles I stood rapt in the wonder   5
of it, came missives from the King, who all-hailed me
Thane of Cawdor – by which title, before, these weird
sisters saluted me; and referred me to the coming on of
time, with "Hail, King that shalt be!" This have I thought
good to deliver thee, my dearest partner of greatness,   10
that thou might'st not lose the dues of rejoicing by being
ignorant of what greatness is promised thee. Lay it to thy
heart, and farewell.'

Glamis thou art, and Cawdor – and shalt be
What thou art promised! – Yet do I fear thy nature.   15
It is too full o' the milk of human kindness
To catch the nearest way. Thou wouldst be great –
Art not without ambition, but without
The illness should attend it. What thou wouldst highly,
That wouldst thou holily – wouldst not play false,   20
And yet wouldst wrongly win. Thou'dst have, great
   Glamis,
That which cries 'Thus thou must do, if thou have it' –
And that which rather thou dost fear to do,
Than wishest should be undone. Hie thee hither! –
That I may pour my spirits in thine ear,   25
And chastise with the valour of my tongue
All that impedes thee from the golden round,
Which fate and metaphysical aid doth seem
To have thee crowned withal. –

Enter a MESSENGER.

                                  What is your tidings?

Lady Macbeth is excited to hear that King Duncan is coming to stay in their castle that very night. Just as she is calling upon evil spirits to assist her in helping Macbeth to kill Duncan, Macbeth arrives.

---Think about---

• Which phrases in Lady Macbeth's two soliloquies (speeches in which she shares her private thoughts with the audience), in lines 14 to 29, and 37 to 53, suggest that she has already decided that they have to kill Duncan?

• Find the examples of language to do with darkness and night in lines 36 to 53, and in Macbeth's speech in Act 1 Scene 4, lines 48 to 53. What does it tell us about the Macbeths? In what ways are they involving the natural world in their plots?

32 informed for preparation: told me to get things ready

34 had the speed of: overtook

36 Give him tending: Look after him
37 raven: Ravens were thought to be messengers of death.

39–40 spirits … on: evil spirits who listen to
40 mortal thoughts: murderous plans
unsex me: take away my female qualities

44 That … nature: so that no pangs of conscience
45 fell: deadly
46 Th' effect and it: my plan and the achievement of it
47 take … gall: exchange my milk for bitter poison
ministers: agents (of evil)
48 sightless substances: invisible bodies
49 wait … mischief: serve the evil in nature
50 pall … dunnest: cover / shroud yourself in the darkest
53 Hold: Stop

56 ignorant present: i.e. not knowing what will happen in the future
57 the instant: what is happening now

59 as he purposes: so he intends

MESSENGER   The King comes here tonight.

LADY MACBETH   Thou'rt mad to say it!   30
Is not thy master with him? – Who, were't so,
Would have informed for preparation.

MESSENGER   So please you, it is true: our Thane is coming.
One of my fellows had the speed of him –
Who, almost dead for breath, had scarcely more   35
Than would make up his message.

LADY MACBETH   Give him tending:
He brings great news. (*Exit* MESSENGER.) The raven
   himself is hoarse
That croaks the fatal entrance of Duncan
Under my battlements. Come, you spirits
That tend on mortal thoughts, unsex me here! –   40
And fill me, from the crown to the toe, top-full
Of direst cruelty! Make thick my blood,
Stop up th' access and passage to remorse –
That no compunctious visitings of nature
Shake my fell purpose, nor keep peace between   45
Th' effect and it! Come to my woman's breasts,
And take my milk for gall, you murdering ministers,
Wherever in your sightless substances
You wait on nature's mischief! Come, thick night,
And pall thee in the dunnest smoke of hell –   50
That my keen knife see not the wound it makes,
Nor heaven peep through the blanket of the dark
To cry, "Hold, hold!"

Enter MACBETH.

                              Great Glamis! Worthy Cawdor!
Greater than both, by the all-hail hereafter!
Thy letters have transported me beyond   55
This ignorant present, and I feel now
The future in the instant.

MACBETH   My dearest love,
Duncan comes here tonight.

LADY MACBETH   And when goes hence?

MACBETH   Tomorrow, as he purposes.

Determined to go through with
the murder of Duncan, Lady
Macbeth tells Macbeth to look
innocent and leave everything
to her.

62–3 **To ... time**: To deceive people, look as
they expect you to look at the time

66 **provided for**: 1 looked after; 2 dealt
with
67 **dispatch**: management
69 **solely ... sway**: absolute power of
being King

70 **Only ... clear**: Just appear innocent
71 **To alter ... fear**: Changing your
expression is always a sign of fear

---**Think about**

• Appearance and reality is a
major theme in this play.
What do the two images in
lines 61 to 65 mean? What
advice is Lady Macbeth
giving her husband?

• What else do Lady
Macbeth's speeches reveal
about the kind of person
she is and the kind of
relationship she has with
Macbeth?

LADY MACBETH	O! – never	
	Shall sun that morrow see!	60

LADY MACBETH   O! – never
            Shall sun that morrow see!   60
            Your face, my thane, is as a book, where men
            May read strange matters. To beguile the time,
            Look like the time. Bear welcome in your eye,
            Your hand, your tongue: look like the innocent flower
            But be the serpent under 't. He that's coming   65
            Must be provided for. And you shall put
            This night's great business into my dispatch –
            Which shall to all our nights and days to come
            Give solely sovereign sway and masterdom.

MACBETH   We will speak further.

LADY MACBETH   Only look up clear.   70
            To alter favour ever is to fear.
            Leave all the rest to me.

                                                    Exeunt.

In this scene ...

- King Duncan arrives at the Macbeths' castle.
- Lady Macbeth welcomes him.

King Duncan arrives at the Macbeths' castle with Banquo and other lords. He admires the castle's beautiful setting and is welcomed by Lady Macbeth.

1 **seat**: situation
2 **Nimbly ... itself:** eagerly shows its sweet qualities

4 **temple-haunting martlet**: house-martin which builds its nest on church walls
   approve: prove
5 **loved mansionry**: favourite home
6 **wooingly**: appealingly
6–7 **jutty ... Buttress**: parts of the stonework that stick out
7 **coign of vantage**: convenient corner
8 **pendent ... cradle**: hanging nest and cradle for its young

11 **our trouble**: a trouble to us
12 **still**: always
13 **yield**: reward

16 **single**: simple
16–17 **contend Against**: i.e. try to match
18 **of old**: in the past
19 **late ... up**: honours added recently
20 **rest your hermits**: will always pray for you, as hermits do

---**Think about**---

- What is there about the characters' comments in lines 1 to 10 that might cause us to recall the Witches' line 'Fair is foul, and foul is fair' (Act 1 Scene 1, line 11)?

- How is dramatic irony used in ths short scene?

Inverness: the approach to Macbeth's castle.

Musicians play a welcoming fanfare (oboes). Torches burn to

light the entrance of the castle.

Enter King DUNCAN, *with* MALCOLM, DONALBAIN, BANQUO,

LENNOX, MACDUFF, ROSS, ANGUS, *and attendants.*

DUNCAN   This castle hath a pleasant seat. The air
Nimbly and sweetly recommends itself
Unto our gentle senses.

BANQUO   This guest of summer,
The temple-haunting martlet, does approve,
By his loved mansionry, that the heaven's breath   5
Smells wooingly here. No jutty, frieze,
Buttress, nor coign of vantage, but this bird
Hath made his pendent bed and procreant cradle.
Where they most breed and haunt, I have observed,
The air is delicate.

Enter LADY MACBETH.

DUNCAN   See, see – our honoured hostess!   10
(*To* LADY MACBETH) The love that follows us sometime
   is our trouble,
Which still we thank as love. Herein I teach you,
How you shall bid God yield us for your pains,
And thank us for your trouble.

LADY MACBETH   All our service,
In every point twice done, and then done double,   15
Were poor and single business, to contend
Against those honours deep and broad wherewith
Your Majesty loads our house. For those of old,
And the late dignities heaped up to them,
We rest your hermits.

Lady Macbeth welcomes
Duncan, and then takes him to
meet Macbeth.

21 **coursed ... heels**: chased closely
behind him
22 **purveyor**: official who rode ahead of
the King
23 **holp**: helped

26 **in count**: in trust / account
27 **make their audit**: present their
financial report
28 **Still**: always

31 **By your leave**: With your permission

Think about

- In Lady Macbeth's reply
(lines 25 to 28) 'count'
means 'account', and
'audit' is a 'financial
report'. What point is she
getting across with this
financial imagery?

- How would you describe
Lady Macbeth's welcome of
Duncan? Which image from
the previous scene might
we recall when we hear her
words to him?

DUNCAN   Where's the Thane of Cawdor?   **20**
We coursed him at the heels, and had a purpose
To be his purveyor. But he rides well –
And his great love, sharp as his spur, hath holp him
To his home before us. Fair and noble hostess,
We are your guest tonight.

LADY MACBETH   Your servants ever   **25**
Have theirs, themselves, and what is theirs in count
To make their audit at your Highness' pleasure –
Still to return your own.

DUNCAN   Give me your hand.
Conduct me to mine host. We love him highly,
And shall continue our graces towards him.   **30**
By your leave, hostess.

Exeunt.

In this scene ...

- Macbeth has left the banquet, tormented by doubts about murdering Duncan.
- When Lady Macbeth comes to fetch him back in to the banquet, he declares that they must not go ahead with the murder.
- Lady Macbeth explains how the blame for the murder can be laid upon Duncan's attendants. She persuades Macbeth to go ahead with the plan.

Macbeth is deeply troubled by what might happen if he kills King Duncan. He considers Duncan's virtues and the powerful reasons for not committing the crime.

Think about

- What are the main points Macbeth is making in his soliloquy (speech in which he shares his private thoughts with the audience)? It will help to think about it in three sections: lines 1 to 7, 7 to 12, and 12 to 28.

---

s.d. **Sewer**: person in charge of servants

1 **If ... done**: i.e. If the killing could be the end of the business

3–4 **trammel ... success**: i.e. prevent any further trouble and achieve success with Duncan's death

5 **the be-all ... here**: the end of the business here on earth

6 **bank ... time**: i.e. this narrow island of life (compared with eternity)

7 **jump ... come**: i.e. risk punishment in the after-life

8 **still ... here**: always receive justice here on earth

8–10 **that ... inventor**: because we give lessons in violence which are then used against us

11–12 **Commends ... lips**: makes us drink our own poison

12 **He's ... trust**: There are two reasons why Duncan should be able to trust me

17 **borne ... meek:** used his power so gently

18 **clear ... office**: free from guilt as a king

20 **taking-off**: murder

22 **Striding the blast**: i.e. joining the storm of horror at the murder
cherubin: angel

23 **sightless couriers**: invisible runners (i.e. the winds)

25–6 **no spur ... intent**: i.e. nothing to drive my intention forward

27–8 **o'erleaps ... other**: jumps too high and falls on the other side

Inverness: inside the castle.

Torch-light. Music is heard from the great hall. A Sewer leads

a line of servants past with dishes for a banquet.

Then enter MACBETH, alone.

MACBETH   If it were done when 'tis done, then 'twere well
It were done quickly. If th' assassination
Could trammel up the consequence, and catch
With his surcease success – that but this blow
Might be the be-all and the end-all here,   5
But here, upon this bank and shoal of time,
We'd jump the life to come. – But in these cases
We still have judgement here – that we but teach
Bloody instructions, which, being taught, return
To plague th' inventor. This even-handed justice   10
Commends th' ingredients of our poisoned chalice
To our own lips. He's here in double trust:
First, as I am his kinsman and his subject,
Strong both against the deed – then, as his host,
Who should against his murderer shut the door,   15
Not bear the knife myself! Besides, this Duncan
Hath borne his faculties so meek, hath been
So clear in his great office, that his virtues
Will plead like angels, trumpet-tongued, against
The deep damnation of his taking-off.   20
And pity, like a naked new-born babe,
Striding the blast, or heaven's cherubin, horsed
Upon the sightless couriers of the air,
Shall blow the horrid deed in every eye,
That tears shall drown the wind! – I have no spur   25
To prick the sides of my intent, but only
Vaulting ambition, which o'erleaps itself
And falls on the other –

Enter LADY MACBETH.

How now? What news?

When Macbeth tells his wife that they must not go ahead with their plan, she accuses him of being a coward. She declares that she would rather kill her own baby than break a promise like this as Macbeth has done.

Think about

- What methods does Lady Macbeth use to persuade her husband to kill Duncan? Think about what arguments she employs in lines 35 to 39, 39 to 45, 49, and 54 to 59.

- How would you describe the language Lady Macbeth uses to persuade her husband? What do Lady Macbeth's speeches reveal about her view of what a 'real man' is? Look at line 49, for example.

29   **supped**: i.e. finished his meal

32–3   **bought … opinions**: earned a fine reputation
34   **worn … gloss**: i.e. enjoyed while they are still new to me

35–6   **Was … yourself**: Was your earlier ambition as shaky as a drunken man
37   **green and pale**: sick (with a hangover)

39   **account**: regard / consider
40–1   **be the … desire**: match your desires with deeds
42   **esteem'st**: value as
ornament of life: i.e. the crown
44   **Letting … would**: not daring to do what you want to do
45   **adage**: proverb
Prithee: I beg you
46   **may become**: is fitting for
47   **none**: i.e. not human

48   **break**: reveal

50   **more … were**: i.e. to be king
51–2   **Nor … both**: Neither the time nor the place were right then, but you were prepared to make them right
53–4   **They … you**: Now that the circumstances are right, that has made you lose your courage
54   **given suck**: fed a baby with my own milk

LADY MACBETH   He has almost supped. Why have you left the chamber?

MACBETH   Hath he asked for me?

LADY MACBETH   Know you not he has?   30

MACBETH   We will proceed no further in this business.
He hath honoured me of late – and I have bought
Golden opinions from all sorts of people,
Which would be worn now in their newest gloss,
Not cast aside so soon.

LADY MACBETH   Was the hope drunk,   35
Wherein you dressed yourself? Hath it slept since?
And wakes it now to look so green and pale
At what it did so freely? From this time
Such I account thy love. Art thou afeard
To be the same in thine own act and valour,   40
As thou art in desire? Wouldst thou have that
Which thou esteem'st the ornament of life,
And live a coward in thine own esteem,
Letting 'I dare not' wait upon 'I would,'
Like the poor cat i'the adage?

MACBETH   Prithee, peace.   45
I dare do all that may become a man –
Who dares do more is none.

LADY MACBETH   What beast was't then
That made you break this enterprise to me?
When you durst do it, then you were a man!
And, to be more than what you were, you would   50
Be so much more the man. Nor time nor place
Did then adhere, and yet you would make both.
They have made themselves, and that their fitness now
Does unmake you. I have given suck, and know
How tender 'tis to love the babe that milks me.   55
I would, while it was smiling in my face,
Have plucked my nipple from his boneless gums,
And dashed the brains out! – had I so sworn as you
Have done to this.

MACBETH   If we should fail, –

Lady Macbeth explains to
Macbeth her plan to blame the
murder of Duncan on his
attendants. Persuaded by his
wife, Macbeth agrees to go
through with the murder.

Think about

• At the end of Act 1 Scene 5
Lady Macbeth said, 'Leave
all the rest to me'. In what
ways has she been true to
her word in this scene?

• What do you make of
Macbeth's reactions to his
wife's arguments? What is
his view now of what they
have to do?

60 **But ... sticking-place**: i.e. just keep
your nerve
62–3 **Whereto ... him**: and he is all the
more likely to sleep deeply after his
hard journey
63 **chamberlains**: attendants in his bed-
chamber
64 **with ... convince**: overpower with
wine and strong drink
65 **warder**: guardian
66 **a fume**: i.e. foggy
receipt of reason: i.e. the brain
67 **limbeck**: flask for impure liquids
swinish: pig-like
70 **put upon**: blame on
71 **spongy**: drink-sodden
72 **quell**: murder
73 **undaunted mettle**: fearless spirit
74 **received**: believed / accepted as the
truth
77 **other**: in any other way
78 **As ... roar**: because we will loudly
express our grief and fury

79 **I am settled**: i.e. My mind is made up
bend up: summon up
80 **Each corporal agent**: all the powers of
my body
81 **mock ... show**: deceive everybody

LADY MACBETH	We fail?
	But screw your courage to the sticking-place **60**
	And we'll not fail! When Duncan is asleep
	(Whereto the rather shall his day's hard journey
	Soundly invite him), his two chamberlains
	Will I with wine and wassail so convince,
	That memory, the warder of the brain, **65**
	Shall be a fume, and the receipt of reason
	A limbeck only. When in swinish sleep
	Their drenchèd natures lie, as in a death,
	What cannot you and I perform upon
	Th' unguarded Duncan? What not put upon **70**
	His spongy officers, who shall bear the guilt
	Of our great quell?
MACBETH	Bring forth men-children only! –
	For thy undaunted mettle should compose
	Nothing but males. Will it not be received,
	When we have marked with blood those sleepy two **75**
	Of his own chamber, and used their very daggers,
	That they have done't?
LADY MACBETH	Who dares receive it other? –
	As we shall make our griefs and clamour roar
	Upon his death?
MACBETH	I am settled – and bend up
	Each corporal agent to this terrible feat. **80**
	Away, and mock the time with fairest show! –
	False face must hide what the false heart doth know.

Exeunt.

Shakespeare's Globe, 2001

Albery Theatre, 2002

RSC, 2004

In this scene ...

- Macbeth tries to test Banquo to see how loyal he might be to him in the future.
- Once Banquo has left, Macbeth has a vision of a dagger stained with blood.
- Macbeth goes to kill Duncan.

Banquo, who is being kept awake by troubling thoughts, is walking outside with his son, Fleance. He meets Macbeth, and tells him how grateful Duncan is for his and Lady Macbeth's hospitality. Banquo mentions their meeting with the Witches.

2   **is down**: has set

4   **husbandry**: good house-keeping
5   **candles**: i.e. stars
6–7   **A heavy … sleep**: I am desperate to sleep, but I don't want to
8–9   **that … repose**: which enter my head when I rest

13   **been … pleasure**: had a particularly enjoyable time
14   **largess**: gifts
       offices: servants' quarters
16   **shut up**: went to bed
17   **in measureless content**: extremely happy
17–19   **Being … wrought**: As we were not prepared for his visit, we could not give as warm a welcome as we would have liked

Think about

- What 'cursèd thoughts' (line 8) are preventing Banquo from sleeping? Look at lines 20 to 21, for example.

- Look at the image in lines 4 to 5. What idea does it convey? What atmosphere does it help to create at the opening of this scene?

Inverness: the castle courtyard.

Enter BANQUO, *and his son* FLEANCE. *A servant carries a burning torch to light their way.*

BANQUO	How goes the night, boy?
FLEANCE	The moon is down. I have not heard the clock.
BANQUO	And she goes down at twelve.
FLEANCE	I take 't, 'tis later, sir.

BANQUO Hold, take my sword. – There's husbandry in heaven:
Their candles are all out. – Take thee that, too.   5
A heavy summons lies like lead upon me,
And yet I would not sleep. Merciful powers! –
Restrain in me the cursèd thoughts that nature
Gives way to in repose! – Give me my sword.

Enter MACBETH, *also with a torch-bearer.*

Who's there?   10

MACBETH A friend.

BANQUO What, sir! Not yet at rest? The King's a-bed.
He hath been in unusual pleasure, and
Sent forth great largess to your offices.
This diamond he greets your wife withal,   15
By the name of most kind hostess – and shut up
In measureless content.

MACBETH   Being unprepared,
Our will became the servant to defect,
Which else should free have wrought.

BANQUO   All's well.
I dreamt last night of the three weird sisters.   20
To you they have showed some truth.

Banquo cautiously says that he is loyal to the King and leaves to go to bed. Left alone, Macbeth suddenly has a vision of a blood-stained dagger.

22 **entreat ... serve**: find a convenient time

24 **At ... leisure**: Whenever it is convenient for you
25 **If ... 'tis**: If you will stay on my side (or follow my advice) when the time comes
26–7 **So ... augment it**: As long as I don't lose honour by trying to gain more
27–8 **still ... clear**: always keep my conscience clear and my loyalty to the King unstained
29 **shall be counselled**: i.e. am willing to listen
Good ... while: Meanwhile, sleep well

Think about

• If you were the director, would you make this conversation between Macbeth and Banquo friendly and warm, or cold and formal? Why?

• How would you represent Macbeth's vision of the dagger in (a) a theatre production; and (b) a film? Think about its position as he sees it, its changing appearance, and the way it behaves. What effect does it have on the audience if we do not see it at all?

36 **have thee not**: can't grasp you
37–8 **sensible ... sight**: able to be touched as well as seen
40 **heat-oppressèd**: feverish
41 **palpable**: apparently touchable
42 **this**: i.e. Macbeth's own dagger
43 **Thou marshall'st**: You direct

45 **Mine ... senses**: Either my eyes are foolish compared with all the other senses
47 **dudgeon**: handle
gouts: drops
49–50 **informs ... eyes**: is making me see things like this

MACBETH	I think not of them.

Yet, when we can entreat an hour to serve,
We would spend it in some words upon that business,
If you would grant the time.

BANQUO   At your kind'st leisure.

MACBETH   If you shall cleave to my consent, when 'tis,   25
It shall make honour for you.

BANQUO   So I lose none
In seeking to augment it, but still keep
My bosom franchised, and allegiance clear,
I shall be counselled.

MACBETH   Good repose the while!

BANQUO   Thanks, sir: the like to you.   30

Exit BANQUO, *with* FLEANCE *and their torch-bearer.*

MACBETH   (*To the servant carrying his torch*)
Go, bid thy mistress, when my drink is ready,
She strike upon the bell. Get thee to bed.

Exit servant.

Is this a dagger which I see before me,
The handle toward my hand?
Come, let me clutch thee. –   35
I have thee not – and yet I see thee still!
Art thou not, fatal vision, sensible
To feeling as to sight? Or art thou but
A dagger of the mind, a false creation,
Proceeding from the heat-oppressèd brain?   40
I see thee yet! – in form as palpable
As this which now I draw.
Thou marshall'st me the way that I was going –
And such an instrument I was to use.
Mine eyes are made the fools o' the other senses,   45
Or else worth all the rest. I see thee still! –
And on thy blade and dudgeon gouts of blood,
Which was not so before. – There's no such thing!
It is the bloody business which informs
Thus to mine eyes. – Now o'er the one half world   50

Afraid of making any noise that might be heard by the sleeping household, Macbeth goes to murder Duncan.

51 **abuse**: deceive / disturb

53 **Hecate**: the goddess of witchcraft
54 **Alarumed**: called into action
    sentinel: sentry / watchman
55 **whose ... watch**: i.e. the wolf's howl is like the watchman's hourly call
56–7 **With ... ghost**: Murder is imagined as the legendary rapist Tarquin, moving silently towards his act of violence.
59 **prate ... whereabout**: gossip about where I am going
60–1 **take ... it**: i.e. break the horrifying silence of the night, which suits what I am going to do
61 **Whiles ... lives**: While I stand here talking about murder, Duncan remains alive
62 **Words ... gives**: words cool down the passion of actions
64 **knell**: funeral bell

Think about

• What does his vision of a dagger suggest about Macbeth's state of mind?

• What image does Macbeth have of 'Murder' in lines 53 to 57? What does this image, and his prayer to 'earth' (lines 57 to 61), tell us about his attitude to what he has to do?

Nature seems dead, and wicked dreams abuse
The curtained sleep. Witchcraft celebrates
Pale Hecate's offerings. And withered Murder,
Alarumed by his sentinel, the wolf,
Whose howl's his watch, thus with his stealthy pace,   **55**
With Tarquin's ravishing strides, towards his design
Moves like a ghost. – Thou sure and firm-set earth,
Hear not my steps, which way they walk, for fear
Thy very stones prate of my whereabout,
And take the present horror from the time,   **60**
Which now suits with it. Whiles I threat, he lives:
Words to the heat of deeds too cold breath gives.

A bell rings.

I go, and it is done. The bell invites me.
Hear it not, Duncan – for it is a knell
That summons thee to heaven or to hell.

                                Exit.

In this scene ...

- Macbeth returns from Duncan's chamber and tells Lady Macbeth how he killed the King.
- Lady Macbeth is appalled to see that Macbeth has brought the bloody daggers away from Duncan's chamber. As he is too frightened to take them back, she does it herself.
- Hearing a knocking at the castle gates, Macbeth and Lady Macbeth go to wash the blood from their hands.

Lady Macbeth has drugged the attendants and has left their daggers ready for Macbeth to use to kill the sleeping King Duncan. Macbeth comes back to report that he has murdered him.

2 **quenched them**: i.e. made them unconscious

3 **fatal bellman**: man who rang the bell before an execution or during a funeral

4 **stern'st**: harshest (because the owl's hoot signals that someone is about to die)

 about it: performing the murder

5–6 **the surfeited ... charge**: Duncan's attendants, who have drunk too much, make a mockery of their job

6 **possets**: late-night alcoholic drinks

7–8 **That ... die**: i.e. so that they seem half dead

11 **Confounds us**: causes our downfall

13 **had done 't**: would have done it

15 **crickets**: Their chirping was thought to foretell death.

Think about

- Sometimes a single line of verse is split between speakers. What is the dramatic effect of breaking up line 16 into four short speeches, three of which are questions? What does it show about the state of mind of the two characters? Think about how the actors might deliver those speeches.

Inside the castle.

Enter LADY MACBETH, *alone.*

LADY MACBETH	That which hath made them drunk hath made me bold.
	What hath quenched them hath given me fire. – Hark!
	– Peace!
	It was the owl that shrieked, the fatal bellman,
	Which gives the stern'st goodnight. He is about it!
	The doors are open, and the surfeited grooms
	Do mock their charge with snores. I have drugged
	their possets –
	That death and nature do contend about them,
	Whether they live or die.

5

MACBETH	*(Calling from a distance)* Who's there? – What, ho!

LADY MACBETH	Alack! I am afraid they have awaked,
	And 'tis not done. The attempt and not the deed
	Confounds us! – Hark! – I laid their daggers ready:
	He could not miss them! – Had he not resembled
	My father as he slept, I had done 't. – My husband!

10

Enter MACBETH *(with two bloodstained daggers).*

MACBETH	I have done the deed. – Didst thou not hear a noise?

LADY MACBETH	I heard the owl scream, and the crickets cry.
	Did not you speak?

15

MACBETH	When?

LADY MACBETH	Now.

MACBETH	As I descended?

LADY MACBETH	Ay.

MACBETH	Hark! Who lies i' the second chamber?

LADY MACBETH	Donalbain.

MACBETH	*(Looking at his bloody hands)* This is a sorry sight.

LADY MACBETH	A foolish thought, to say a sorry sight.

Macbeth is greatly shaken
because he could not say
'Amen' and because he heard a
voice tell him that he would
never be able to sleep again.
Lady Macbeth is shocked that
he has brought the blood-
stained daggers away with him.

Think about

• If you were directing a film
of *Macbeth*, would you
show the scene in which
Macbeth murders Duncan
(as Macbeth describes it in
lines 19 to 40)? Think about
what you would gain by
showing it, and what you
would lose.

• In what ways have Macbeth
and Lady Macbeth already
been affected by the murder
of the King?

21 **That**: so that
22 **addressed them**: got ready

23 **lodged together**: sleeping in the same
room

25 **As**: as if
hangman's hands: executioner's bloody
hands

28 **wherefore**: why

31 **After**: in

32 **Methought**: It seemed to me

34 **ravelled sleave**: tangled thread
35 **sore … bath**: i.e. sleep eases the aches
caused by hard work
36 **Balm of**: soothing oil for
second course: the main course in a
meal

39 **Glamis … Cawdor**: Macbeth is Thane
of Glamis and Thane of Cawdor.

41 **unbend**: weaken
43 **brainsickly**: feverishly
44 **filthy witness**: evidence of horrible
deeds

MACBETH	There's one did laugh in's sleep, and one cried 'Murder!', 20
	That they did wake each other. I stood and heard them.
	But they did say their prayers, and addressed them
	Again to sleep.
LADY MACBETH	There are two lodged together.
MACBETH	One cried, 'God bless us!' and 'Amen', the other –
	As they had seen me with these hangman's hands. 25
	Listening their fear, I could not say 'Amen',
	When they did say 'God bless us!'
LADY MACBETH	Consider it not so deeply.
MACBETH	But wherefore could not I pronounce 'Amen'?
	I had most need of blessing, and 'Amen'
	Stuck in my throat.
LADY MACBETH	These deeds must not be thought 30
	After these ways: so, it will make us mad.
MACBETH	Methought I heard a voice cry, 'Sleep no more! –
	Macbeth does murder sleep!' – the innocent sleep –
	Sleep that knits up the ravelled sleave of care,
	The death of each day's life, sore labour's bath, 35
	Balm of hurt minds, great nature's second course,
	Chief nourisher in life's feast –
LADY MACBETH	What do you mean?
MACBETH	Still it cried, 'Sleep no more!' to all the house:
	'Glamis hath murdered sleep – and therefore Cawdor
	Shall sleep no more. Macbeth shall sleep no more!' 40
LADY MACBETH	Who was it that thus cried? Why, worthy thane,
	You do unbend your noble strength, to think
	So brainsickly of things. Go, get some water,
	And wash this filthy witness from your hand. –
	Why did you bring these daggers from the place? 45
	They must lie there! Go, carry them, and smear
	The sleepy grooms with blood.
MACBETH	I'll go no more.
	I am afraid to think what I have done.
	Look on't again I dare not.

Lady Macbeth angrily takes the daggers back herself because Macbeth refuses to. They hear a knocking at the castle gates. They go to wash the blood from their hands, Macbeth already regretting what he has done.

Think about

- What does Macbeth's reaction in lines 14 to 40 to the sounds he has heard (or thinks he has heard) suggest about his state of mind? Look at line 55, for example.

- Lady Macbeth says, 'A little water clears us of this deed' (line 64). What does she mean? Will she be proved right, do you think?

- What do you think Macbeth means by 'To know my deed, 'twere best not know myself' (line 70)?

49 **Infirm of purpose**: Weak-willed man

51–2 **'tis … devil**: i.e. only children are frightened of pictures

53 **gild**: paint (with gold)

54 **seem their guilt**: i.e. look as though they have committed the murder

54 **Whence … knocking**: Where's that knocking coming from

56 **They … eyes**: i.e. he wants to pull his eyes out so that they can no longer see his bloody hands

57 **Neptune**: the Roman god of the sea

58–60 **this … red**: my hand is more likely to turn the countless green seas blood red

62 **white**: i.e. cowardly

63 **Retire … chamber**: Let's go to our bedroom

65 **constancy … unattended**: firmness of purpose has deserted you

67–8 **lest … watchers**: in case people call us and realise we have been up and awake

71 **I … couldst**: I wish you could

LADY MACBETH   Infirm of purpose!
              Give me the daggers! The sleeping and the dead   50
              Are but as pictures: 'tis the eye of childhood
              That fears a painted devil. If he do bleed,
              I'll gild the faces of the grooms withal,
              For it must seem their guilt.

                                                                  Exit.

      A knocking is heard.

MACBETH   Whence is that knocking? –
              How is't with me, when every noise appals me?   55
              What hands are here? Ha! They pluck out mine eyes!
              Will all great Neptune's ocean wash this blood
              Clean from my hand? No – this my hand will rather
              The multitudinous seas incarnadine,
              Making the green one red.   60

      Re-enter LADY MACBETH.

LADY MACBETH My hands are of your colour – but I shame
              To wear a heart so white! (*Knocking heard again*)
                  I hear a knocking
              At the south entry. Retire we to our chamber.
              A little water clears us of this deed:
              How easy is it then! Your constancy   65
              Hath left you unattended. (*Knocking again*) Hark! –
                  more knocking.
              Get on your night-gown, lest occasion call us,
              And show us to be watchers. – Be not lost
              So poorly in your thoughts!

MACBETH   To know my deed, 'twere best not know myself.   70

      Knocking heard again.

              Wake Duncan with thy knocking! I would thou couldst!

                                                                Exeunt.

Battersea Arts Centre, 2000

RSC, 1993

RSC, 1999

RSC, 1996

In this scene ...

- The castle porter opens the gates to Macduff and Lennox and jokes with them.
- Having gone to wake the King, Macduff discovers the murder. Duncan's sons, Malcolm and Donalbain, are told of their father's death.
- As Macbeth is explaining that he killed the attendants because he was furious that they had killed Duncan, his wife faints.
- Malcolm and Donalbain, fearing for their safety, decide to flee.

The castle porter imagines himself to be the porter of the gates of hell, welcoming in various types of sinner. He opens the gates to let in Macduff and Lennox.

Think about

- What effect does the entrance of the Porter, a comic character, have at this point in the play?

- In what ways is the Porter's opening speech both comic and serious?

2 **old**: plenty of

4 **Beelzebub**: the devil
5 **plenty**: a good harvest
   time-server: somebody who 1 depends on the seasons; 2 will serve time in hell
6 **napkins**: handkerchiefs (to mop up the sweat in hell)
7–8 **other devil**: probably Satan
8 **equivocator**: someone who deceives by telling half-truths
9 **swear ... scale**: balance up the scales of Justice by arguing on both sides
10 **treason**: betraying your King or country
14 **stealing ... hose**: i.e. using less cloth than the customers had paid for
14–15 **roast your goose**: 1 heat your flat-iron; 2 sweat out your diseased body
18–19 **primrose ... bonfire**: i.e. attractive path to hell
20 **Anon**: I'm coming
   remember: i.e. give a tip to
21 **ere**: before
23 **carousing ... cock**: drinking until three in the morning
24 **provoker**: encourager
26 **Marry**: Indeed (By Saint Mary)
   nose-painting: getting a red nose (through drink)
   Lechery: Wanting to have sex
28 **takes ... performance**: i.e. makes you incapable of having sex

The castle courtyard.

Knocking heard again.

Enter the PORTER *of the gate.*

PORTER   Here's a knocking indeed! If a man were porter of hell-gate, he should have old turning the key. (*Knocking again*) Knock, knock, knock. Who's there, i' the name of Beelzebub? – Here's a farmer that hanged himself on the expectation of plenty. Come in, time-server. Have   5
napkins enough about you: here you'll sweat for it. (*Knocking again*) Knock, knock! Who's there, i' the other devil's name? – 'Faith, here's an equivocator that could swear in both the scales against either scale – who committed treason enough for God's sake, yet could not   10
equivocate to heaven. O, come in, equivocator! (*Knocking again*) Knock, knock, knock. Who's there? – 'Faith, here's an English tailor, come hither for stealing out of a French hose. Come in, tailor! Here you may roast your goose. (*Knocking again*) Knock, knock.   15
Never at quiet! What are you? – But this place is too cold for hell. I'll devil-porter it no further. I had thought to have let in some of all professions that go the primrose way to the everlasting bonfire. (*Knocking again*) Anon, anon! I pray you, remember the porter.   20

He opens the gate.

Enter MACDUFF *and* LENNOX.

MACDUFF   Was it so late, friend, ere you went to bed,
That you do lie so late?

PORTER   'Faith, sir, we were carousing till the second cock – and drink, sir, is a great provoker of three things.

MACDUFF   What three things does drink especially provoke?   25

PORTER   Marry, sir, nose-painting, sleep and urine. Lechery, sir, it provokes and unprovokes: it provokes the desire, but it takes away the performance. Therefore, much drink may

The Porter jokes with Macduff
and Lennox about the effects of
alcohol. Macbeth enters and
tells Macduff where the King's
room is, because Duncan had
asked Macduff to wake him.

29 **equivocator with**: deceiver of
30 **mars**: ruins
30–2 **it sets ... stand to**: i.e. it gives him a
sexual appetite but makes him
incapable of satisfying it
33 **giving him the lie:** 1 deceiving him;
2 making him lie down; 3 making him
urinate
35 **i' the ... o' me**: 1 by lying to my face;
2 by being poured down my throat
requited him: paid him back
37 **took up my legs**: i.e. made me fall over
made a shift: managed
38 **cast**: 1 throw (as in wrestling);
2 throw up

43 **timely**: early
44 **slipped**: missed

45–6 **joyful ... one**: i.e. because Macbeth
has been pleased to have the King in
his castle, even though the visit has
caused extra work
47 **The ... pain**: Work that we enjoy is a
cure for any hardship it causes
49 **my limited service**: what I was asked
to do

50 **Goes ... hence**: Is the King leaving

---Think about---

• The Porter imagines
welcoming an 'equivocator'
to hell (lines 8 to 11) and
says that drink is 'an
equivocator with lechery'
(lines 29 to 33). Where else
in the play do we
encounter equivocating –
the telling of half-truths?

be said to be an equivocator with lechery: it makes him
and it mars him; it sets him on, and it takes him off; it   30
persuades him, and disheartens him; makes him stand
to, and not stand to. In conclusion, equivocates him in
a sleep, and, giving him the lie, leaves him.

MACDUFF   I believe drink gave thee the lie last night.

PORTER   That it did, sir, i' the very throat o' me. But I requited   35
             him for his lie – and, I think, being too strong for him,
             though he took up my legs sometime, yet I made a shift
             to cast him.

MACDUFF   Is thy master stirring?

Enter MACBETH.

             Our knocking has awaked him: here he comes.   40

LENNOX   Good morrow, noble sir!

MACBETH   Good morrow, both!

                                        Exit the PORTER.

MACDUFF   Is the King stirring, worthy Thane?

MACBETH   Not yet.

MACDUFF   He did command me to call timely on him:
             I have almost slipped the hour.

MACBETH   I'll bring you to him.

MACDUFF   I know this is a joyful trouble to you;   45
             But yet 'tis one.

MACBETH   The labour we delight in physics pain.
             This is the door.

MACDUFF   I'll make so bold to call,
             For 'tis my limited service.

                                                        Exit.

LENNOX   Goes the King hence today?

MACBETH   He does. – He did appoint so.   50

As Lennox is describing the
strange, unnatural events of the
previous night, Macduff comes
back crying out in horror
because he has discovered
Duncan's murder.

51 **unruly**: wild and stormy

53 **Lamentings**: cries of misery
54 **prophesying ... terrible**: forecasting in
a horrifying way
55 **dire ... events**: terrible confusion and
chaos
56 **New hatched to**: born out of
obscure bird: owl
57 **Clamoured**: i.e. hooted
59–60 **My young ... it**: I cannot recall a night
like it in my young life

62 **conceive**: imagine

63 **Confusion**: Destruction
64 **sacrilegious**: unholy
ope: open
65 **Lord's anointed temple**: i.e. the King's
body

69 **Gorgon**: In Greek mythology, anyone
who looked at the Gorgon was turned
to stone.

73 **downy**: comfortable
death's counterfeit: i.e. sleep
75 **The ... image**: a sight as terrifying as
the Last Judgement (when the souls of
the dead will finally be judged)
76 **sprites**: spirits
77 **countenance**: 1 face; 2 be in keeping
with

Think about

• What impact might
Lennox's speech (lines 51 to
58) have had in
Shakespeare's time? Think
about lines 63 to 66 and
the beliefs Shakespeare's
audience would have had
about omens and kingship.

LENNOX	The night has been unruly. Where we lay,
	Our chimneys were blown down – and, as they say,
	Lamentings heard i' the air – strange screams of death,
	And prophesying with accents terrible
	Of dire combustion, and confused events,	55
	New hatched to the woeful time. The obscure bird
	Clamoured the livelong night. Some say the earth
	Was feverous, and did shake.

| MACBETH | 'Twas a rough night. |

| LENNOX | My young remembrance cannot parallel |
| | A fellow to it. | 60 |

Re-enter MACDUFF.

| MACDUFF | O horror! Horror! Horror! Tongue, nor heart, |
| | Cannot conceive, nor name thee! |

| MACBETH and LENNOX | What's the matter? |

MACDUFF	Confusion now hath made his masterpiece!
	Most sacrilegious murder hath broke ope
	The Lord's anointed temple, and stole thence	65
	The life o' the building!

| MACBETH | What is't you say? – the life? |

| LENNOX | Mean you his majesty? |

MACDUFF	Approach the chamber, and destroy your sight
	With a new Gorgon. – Do not bid me speak:
	See, and then speak yourselves. –

Exit MACBETH, *with* LENNOX.

	Awake! Awake! –	70
	Ring the alarum-bell! – Murder and treason!
	Banquo and Donalbain! Malcolm! Awake!
	Shake off this downy sleep, death's counterfeit,
	And look on death itself! – Up, up, and see
	The great doom's image! – Malcolm! Banquo!	75
	As from your graves rise up, and walk like sprites
	To countenance this horror!

Ringing of the alarm bell is heard.

Lady Macbeth and Banquo are told that Duncan has been murdered. Macbeth expresses shock. When Duncan's sons, Malcolm and Donalbain, enter they are told that their father has been killed.

78 **to parley**: for a conference

81–2 **The repetition ... fell**: Reporting it to a woman would kill her

85 **prithee**: beg you

87 **chance**: happening

89 **serious in mortality**: important in human life (or death)
90 **toys**: trivial things
    renown and grace: fame and good deeds
91 **drawn**: taken from the barrel
    the mere lees: only the dregs
92 **vault**: wine cellar, i.e. the world
    brag of: boast about
93 **What is amiss**: What's wrong
94 **The spring ... blood**: i.e. your father
95 **stopped**: i.e. dead

---Think about---

• If you were the director, how would you ask the actors playing (a) Lady Macbeth; (b) Banquo; (c) Macbeth; and (d) Macduff, to react when they hear of the murder?

• What idea is Macbeth conveying in lines 91 to 92? How effective is the image he uses in getting that idea across?

Enter LADY MACBETH.

LADY MACBETH   What's the business,
                  That such a hideous trumpet calls to parley
                  The sleepers of the house? Speak, speak!

MACDUFF   O gentle lady,
                  'Tis not for you to hear what I can speak.   80
                  The repetition, in a woman's ear,
                  Would murder as it fell. –

Enter BANQUO.

                                        O Banquo! Banquo!
                  Our royal master's murdered!

LADY MACBETH   Woe, alas!
                  What! In our house?

BANQUO   Too cruel anywhere!
                  Dear Duff, I prithee contradict thyself   85
                  And say it is not so.

Re-enter MACBETH *and* LENNOX.

MACBETH   Had I but died an hour before this chance,
                  I had lived a blessèd time – for, from this instant,
                  There's nothing serious in mortality.
                  All is but toys: renown and grace is dead –   90
                  The wine of life is drawn, and the mere lees
                  Is left this vault to brag of.

Enter MALCOLM *and* DONALBAIN.

DONALBAIN   What is amiss?

MACBETH   You are, and do not know it.
                  The spring, the head, the fountain of your blood
                  Is stopped: the very source of it is stopped.   95

MACDUFF   Your royal father's murdered.

MALCOLM   O! By whom?

Lennox says that it seems that Duncan was killed by the attendants in his room. Macbeth claims that he killed the attendants in his fury. As he goes on to describe how he saw the murdered Duncan, Lady Macbeth faints. Malcolm and Donalbain privately share their fears for their own safety.

Think about

- In a performance, Lady Macbeth's faint (line 114) can be acted as though either genuine or fake. If you were the director, how would you want to show it, and why?

- Macbeth's language here is complex and full of images, but the language of the other characters is more straightforward. What could account for this contrast?

98 **badged**: marked, i.e. blood was the 'badge' which showed that they were murderers
100 **distracted**: behaved as if mad

103 **Wherefore**: Why

104 **temperate**: level-headed

106–7 **The expedition … reason**: My passionate love for the King made me act hastily, before reason could make me stop and think
108 **laced**: i.e. streaked
109 **breach**: gaping hole
111 **Steeped**: dyed
colours … trade: i.e. blood-red
112 **Unmannerly … gore**: indecently clothed with blood
refrain: restrain himself
114 **make's**: make his

116 **That … ours**: when we are the ones most closely affected by what's happened
118 **auger-hole**: tiny drill-hole
119–20 **Our … brewed**: i.e. We are not ready to weep yet

121 **Upon … motion**: i.e. ready to show itself

122 **our … hid**: i.e. got dressed

125 **scruples**: doubts

LENNOX	Those of his chamber, as it seemed, had done it.
	Their hands and faces were all badged with blood:
	So were their daggers, which, unwiped, we found
	Upon their pillows. They stared, and were distracted. 100
	No man's life was to be trusted with them.

| MACBETH | O, yet I do repent me of my fury – |
| | That I did kill them. |

| MACDUFF | Wherefore did you so? |

MACBETH	Who can be wise, amazed, temperate and furious,
	Loyal and neutral, in a moment? No man! 105
	The expedition of my violent love
	Outran the pauser reason. – Here lay Duncan,
	His silver skin laced with his golden blood!
	And his gashed stabs looked like a breach in nature
	For ruin's wasteful entrance. There, the murderers, 110
	Steeped in the colours of their trade! – their daggers
	Unmannerly breeched with gore. Who could refrain,
	That had a heart to love – and in that heart
	Courage, to make's love known?

| LADY MACBETH | (*Fainting*) Help me hence, ho! |

| MACDUFF | Look to the lady! |

| MALCOLM | (*Aside to* DONALBAIN) Why do we hold our tongues,   115 |
| | That most may claim this argument for ours? |

DONALBAIN	(*Aside to* MALCOLM) What should be spoken
	Here – where our fate, hid in an auger-hole,
	May rush and seize us? Let's away. Our tears
	Are not yet brewed.

| MALCOLM | (*Aside to* DONALBAIN) Nor our strong sorrow   120 |
| | Upon the foot of motion. |

| BANQUO | Look to the lady! – |

LADY MACBETH *is helped away.*

	And when we have our naked frailties hid
	That suffer in exposure, let us meet,
	And question this most bloody piece of work,
	To know it further. Fears and scruples shake us. 125

When everyone else has gone
to get dressed, Malcolm and
Donalbain discuss what to do.
Malcolm decides to flee to
England, Donalbain to Ireland.
Malcolm fears that there will be
more killings.

Think about

• What does Banquo's
response to the situation
reveal about him (lines 121
to 128)?

• Do you think Malcolm and
Donalbain have a good
idea about who murdered
their father? Why?

• What do you think about
Malcolm and Donalbain's
decision to flee, and for
Malcolm to go to England,
Donalbain to Ireland?

126–8 **In ... malice:** I put myself under God's
protection and, relying on God, I will
fight against the hidden purposes of
wicked traitors

129 **briefly**: quickly
put ... readiness: 1 get properly
dressed; 2 adopt a warlike frame of
mind

131 **consort**: keep company
132 **office**: action
133 **false**: deceitful
134–5 **Our ... safer**: We will be safer if we
are not together
136–7 **the near ... bloody**: the more closely
we are related to these deceitful
people, the more chance we have of
being murdered
137–8 **shaft ... lighted**: arrow has not yet hit
its target
140 **dainty of leave-taking**: fussy about
saying goodbye properly
141 **shift away**: slip away
141–2 **There's ... left**: When there are
merciless people around, slipping
away is justifiable

In the great hand of God I stand – and thence
Against the undivulged pretence I fight
Of treasonous malice.

MACDUFF   And so do I.

ALL   So all.

MACBETH   Let's briefly put on manly readiness,
And meet i' the hall together.

ALL   Well contented.   130

Exit MACBETH, *with* MACDUFF, BANQUO *and* LENNOX.
MALCOLM *and* DONALBAIN *remain.*

MALCOLM   What will you do? Let's not consort with them.
To show an unfelt sorrow is an office
Which the false man does easy. I'll to England.

DONALBAIN To Ireland, I. Our separated fortune
Shall keep us both the safer. Where we are   135
There's daggers in men's smiles: the near in blood,
The nearer bloody.

MALCOLM   This murderous shaft that's shot
Hath not yet lighted, and our safest way
Is to avoid the aim. Therefore to horse,
And let us not be dainty of leave-taking,   140
But shift away. There's warrant in that theft
Which steals itself, when there's no mercy left.

Exeunt.

Birmingham Repertory Theatre, 1995

Queen's Theatre, 1999

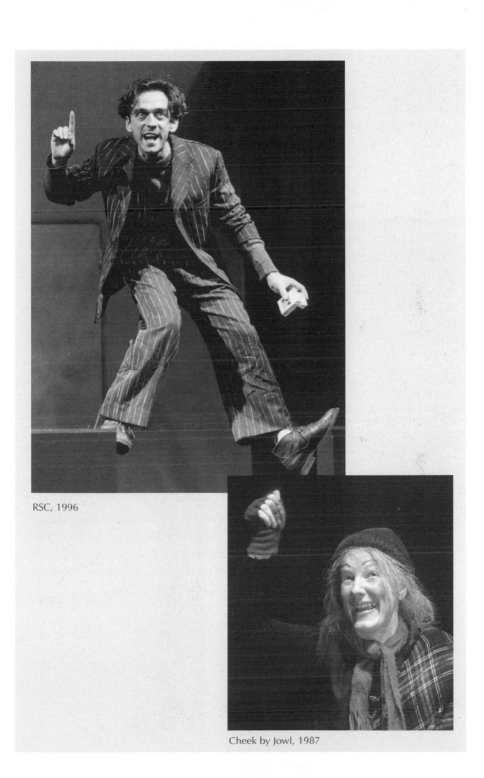

RSC, 1996

Cheek by Jowl, 1987

In this scene ...

- An old man and Ross discuss the strange, unnatural events which have followed the killing of Duncan.
- Macduff joins them. He reports that Duncan's sons, Malcolm and Donalbain, are said to have bribed their father's attendants to kill him.
- While Macduff decides to return to his castle in Fife, Ross goes to see Macbeth crowned as King.

Ross and an old man talk about the disturbing unnatural events that have followed King Duncan's murder.

1 **Threescore and ten**: Seventy years

2 **volume**: space

3 **sore**: dreadful

4 **trifled ... knowings**: made everything I have experienced before seem trivial
father: a term of respect to an old man

5–6 **Thou ... stage**: i.e. the heavens, as though disturbed by men's actions, are now threatening the earth

7 **travelling lamp**: i.e. the sun

8 **Is't ... shame**: Is it the superior power of night, or is the day hiding its face in shame

9 **entomb**: cover, as though in a dark tomb

12 **towering ... place**: rising to her highest point

13 **by ... killed**: i.e. the owl, which normally preyed only on small creatures, attacked a (fiercer) falcon

15 **minions of their race**: the best of their breed

17 **Contending ... obedience**: rebelling against their training
as: as if

Think about

- Which other happenings in the play are 'against nature'? Look back at Act 1 Scene 3, lines 137 to 138, and Act 1 Scene 5, lines 39 to 53, for example. What is causing them?

- In Shakespeare's theatre, the 'heavens' – stars, moon and sun – were painted on the underside of the canopy over the stage. What is Ross suggesting by his playhouse imagery in lines 5 and 6?

Inverness: outside the castle.

Enter ROSS, *with an* OLD MAN.

OLD MAN   Threescore and ten I can remember well –
          Within the volume of which time I have seen
          Hours dreadful and things strange. But this sore night
          Hath trifled former knowings.

ROSS   Ha, good father,
          Thou see'st the heavens, as troubled with man's act,   5
          Threatens his bloody stage. By the clock 'tis day,
          And yet dark night strangles the travelling lamp.
          Is't night's predominance, or the day's shame,
          That darkness does the face of earth entomb,
          When living light should kiss it?

OLD MAN   'Tis unnatural –   10
          Even like the deed that's done. On Tuesday last,
          A falcon, towering in her pride of place,
          Was by a mousing owl hawked at, and killed.

ROSS   And Duncan's horses (a thing most strange and certain),
          Beauteous and swift, the minions of their race,   15
          Turned wild in nature, broke their stalls, flung out,
          Contending 'gainst obedience, as they would make
          War with mankind.

OLD MAN   'Tis said, they ate each other.

ROSS   They did so, to th' amazement of mine eyes,
          That looked upon it. –

          Enter MACDUFF.

                              Here comes the good Macduff. –   20
          How goes the world, sir, now?

MACDUFF   Why, see you not?

ROSS   Is't known who did this more than bloody deed?

MACDUFF   Those that Macbeth hath slain.

Macduff says that the attendants are reported to have killed Duncan on Malcolm's and Donalbain's orders. He says that Macbeth has already gone to Scone to be crowned, but that he himself is not going to attend the coronation.

24 **What ... pretend**: What could they hope to gain by it
suborned: bribed to commit the crime

27 **'Gainst nature still**: Yet another example of unnatural events

28–9 **Thriftless ... means**: Pointless ambition, which will gobble up the body that gives you life

29 **like**: likely that

30 **sovereignty**: title of King

31 **named**: chosen as King
Scone: The place where Scottish kings were crowned.

32 **invested**: crowned

33 **Colme-kill**: The island of Iona, where Scottish kings were buried.

36 **thither**: go there (to the coronation)

37 **Adieu**: Goodbye

40 **benison**: blessing

Think about

• What do you think Macduff feels about the theory that Duncan's sons bribed his attendants to kill their father?

• What evidence is there that Macduff is unhappy at the idea of Macbeth becoming King?

• What does Macduff mean in lines 37 to 38? How effective is the clothing imagery he uses in getting the point across?

ROSS	Alas, the day!
	What good could they pretend?
MACDUFF	They were suborned.
	Malcolm and Donalbain, the King's two sons,
	Are stol'n away and fled – which puts upon them
	Suspicion of the deed.
ROSS	'Gainst nature still!
	Thriftless ambition, that wilt ravin up
	Thine own life's means! – Then 'tis most like
	The sovereignty will fall upon Macbeth.
MACDUFF	He is already named, and gone to Scone
	To be invested.
ROSS	Where is Duncan's body?
MACDUFF	Carried to Colme-kill –
	The sacred storehouse of his predecessors,
	And guardian of their bones.
ROSS	Will you to Scone?
MACDUFF	No, cousin: I'll to Fife.
ROSS	Well, I will thither.
MACDUFF	Well, may you see things well done there. – Adieu! –
	Lest our old robes sit easier than our new!
ROSS	Farewell, father.
OLD MAN	God's benison go with you – and with those
	That would make good of bad, and friends of foes!

25

30

35

40

Exeunt.

In this scene ...

- Banquo privately says that he is suspicious of Macbeth.
- Macbeth and Lady Macbeth – now King and Queen – greet Banquo. Macbeth checks on Banquo's plans to go riding that afternoon.
- Macbeth privately expresses his fears about Banquo. He knows that Banquo is a good man, and he cannot forget the Witches' prophecy that Banquo's descendants will be kings.
- He persuades two murderers to kill Banquo and his son, Fleance.

Banquo expresses his fear that Macbeth must have murdered Duncan. He wonders whether the Witches' prophecy for himself will come true. To gain information about Banquo's movements, Macbeth asks him whether he plans to go riding that afternoon.

1 **it**: i.e. the crown

3 **Thou ... foully**: you played a very dirty game

4 **It ... posterity**: the crown would not be passed on to your descendants

6 **them**: i.e. the Witches

7 **shine**: are brilliantly fulfilled

8 **verities ... good**: things that have come true for you

9 **oracles**: i.e. like the ancient priestesses who foretold what would happen

13 **all-thing unbecoming**: completely inappropriate

14 **solemn**: ceremonial

17–18 **with ... knit**: tied with a knot which cannot be broken

20 **else**: otherwise

21 **still**: always
    grave and prosperous: serious and profitable

22 **council**: meeting of the King and his advisors

Think about

- If you were the director, how would you ask the actor playing Banquo to deliver lines 1 to 10? Think about whether you would show him as a good man, deeply troubled by fears that Macbeth has murdered the King, or as an ambitious man who hopes that the prophecy made to him will now come true.

Forres: inside the palace.

Enter BANQUO, *alone.*

BANQUO
Thou hast it now – King, Cawdor, Glamis, all,
As the weird women promised; and, I fear,
Thou playedst most foully for't. Yet it was said,
It should not stand in thy posterity;
But that myself should be the root and father   5
Of many kings. If there come truth from them
(As upon thee, Macbeth, their speeches shine),
Why, by the verities on thee made good,
May they not be my oracles as well,
And set me up in hope? But, hush: no more.   10

Trumpet fanfare. Enter MACBETH, *as King,* LADY MACBETH, *as*
Queen, with LENNOX, ROSS, *other Lords, and attendants.*

MACBETH
Here's our chief guest.

LADY MACBETH
                              If he had been forgotten,
It had been as a gap in our great feast,
And all-thing unbecoming.

MACBETH
(*To* BANQUO) Tonight we hold a solemn supper, sir,
And I'll request your presence.

BANQUO
                              Let your Highness   15
Command upon me, to the which my duties
Are with a most indissoluble tie
For ever knit.

MACBETH
Ride you this afternoon?

BANQUO
                              Ay, my good lord.

MACBETH
We should have else desired your good advice   20
(Which still hath been both grave and prosperous)
In this day's council. But we'll take tomorrow.
Is't far you ride?

Macbeth asks Banquo whether his son, Fleance, will be going riding with him. Macbeth sends Lady Macbeth and the others away and gives voice to his fears about Banquo.

25   **go … better**: if my horse doesn't go faster

26–7 **become … twain**: have to take up an hour or two of the night

27   **Fail not**: Don't miss

29   **bloody cousins**: i.e. Malcolm and Donalbain (who, according to Macbeth, murdered their father)
      bestowed: settled

31   **parricide**: killing of their father

32   **strange invention**: absurd lies

33   **therewithal**: in addition
      cause: business

34   **Craving us jointly**: which we need to deal with together
      Hie you: Hurry

36   **our … upon 's**: it is time for us to go

40   **be … time**: pass the time as he wishes

41   **society**: being with each other

43   **while**: until

44   **Sirrah**: i.e. You, there!

44–5 **Attend … pleasure**: Are those men waiting to see me

46   **without**: outside

47   **thus**: i.e. King

49   **royalty of nature**: natural nobility

51   **to … temper**: as well as that fearless spirit

52   **valour**: courage

Think about

- Remember Lady Macbeth's advice to Macbeth to 'look like the innocent flower But be the serpent under 't' (Act 1 Scene 5, lines 64 to 65). Which three 'innocent' questions does Macbeth throw into his conversation with Banquo here?

BANQUO	As far, my lord, as will fill up the time
	'Twixt this and supper. Go not my horse the better, 25
	I must become a borrower of the night
	For a dark hour or twain.
MACBETH	Fail not our feast.
BANQUO	My lord, I will not.
MACBETH	We hear our bloody cousins are bestowed
	In England and in Ireland – not confessing 30
	Their cruel parricide, filling their hearers
	With strange invention. But of that tomorrow,
	When, therewithal, we shall have cause of state
	Craving us jointly. Hie you to horse. Adieu,
	Till you return at night. Goes Fleance with you? 35
BANQUO	Ay, my good lord: our time does call upon 's.
MACBETH	I wish your horses swift, and sure of foot;
	And so I do commend you to their backs.
	Farewell.

Exit BANQUO.

(*To the other lords*) Let every man be master of his time 40
Till seven at night. To make society
The sweeter welcome, we will keep ourself
Till supper-time alone: while then, God be with you.

Exit LADY MACBETH, *with* LENNOX, ROSS, *Lords, and attendants.*

(*To a servant*) Sirrah, a word with you. Attend those men
Our pleasure? 45

SERVANT	They are, my lord, without the palace gate.
MACBETH	Bring them before us. (*Exit* SERVANT, *leaving Macbeth alone.*) – To be thus is nothing,
	But to be safely thus! – Our fears in Banquo
	Stick deep – and in his royalty of nature
	Reigns that which would be feared. 'Tis much he dares – 50
	And, to that dauntless temper of his mind,
	He hath a wisdom that doth guide his valour
	To act in safety. There is none but he

Macbeth is tormented by the Witches' prophecy that Banquo's descendants will be kings of Scotland, and he has decided to take action. He calls in two murderers and convinces them that Banquo has always been their enemy.

Think about

- Look at Macbeth's speech (lines 47 to 71). What exactly are his fears about Banquo? What does Macbeth fear might have resulted from his murder of Duncan? How does he decide to deal with these fears?

54–5 under ... rebuked: my guardian spirit is subdued by Banquo's
56 chid: spoke harshly to
58 bade: asked

60–1 fruitless ... sceptre: i.e. no sons of Macbeth will become kings
61 gripe: grip
62 Thence ... hand: to be torn from it by someone who is not one of my descendants
64 issue: descendants
filed: polluted
66 rancours: bitter thoughts
vessel ... peace: my otherwise peaceful mind
67 mine eternal jewel: my immortal soul
68 common ... man: i.e. the devil
70 Rather than so: Instead of letting that happen
list: tournament
71 champion ... utterance: i.e. Macbeth is determined to fight the fate which has said that Banquo's offspring will be kings

76 he: i.e. Banquo
76–7 which ... fortune: i.e. who stopped you enjoying the life you deserved
78 made ... you: showed you convincingly
79 passed in probation: went over the proof
80 borne ... instruments: deceived, obstructed, and what methods he used
81 wrought with them: was involved
82–3 To ... Banquo: i.e. which even a half-wit or madman could see was Banquo's doing

Whose being I do fear – and under him
My genius is rebuked, as, it is said,   55
Mark Antony's was by Caesar. He chid the sisters
When first they put the name of king upon me,
And bade them speak to him. Then, prophet-like,
They hailed him father to a line of kings.
Upon my head they placed a fruitless crown,   60
And put a barren sceptre in my gripe,
Thence to be wrenched with an unlineal hand,
No son of mine succeeding. If 't be so,
For *Banquo's* issue have I filed my mind –
For them the gracious Duncan have I murdered;   65
Put rancours in the vessel of my peace
Only for them – and mine eternal jewel
Given to the common enemy of man,
To make them kings, the seed of Banquo kings!
Rather than so, come, Fate, into the list,   70
And champion me to the utterance! – Who's there? –

Re-enter the SERVANT, *bringing two* MURDERERS.

(*To the* SERVANT) Now go to the door, and stay there
    till we call.

Exit SERVANT.

Was it not yesterday we spoke together?

MURDERER 1   It was, so please your Highness.

MACBETH   Well then, now
Have you considered of my speeches? Know   75
That it was *he*, in the times past, which held you
So under fortune, which you thought had been
Our innocent self. This I made good to you
In our last conference; passed in probation with you
How you were borne in hand; how crossed, the
    instruments;   80
Who wrought with them – and all things else, that
    might
To half a soul, and to a notion crazed,
Say, 'Thus did Banquo'.

MURDERER 1   You made it known to us.

Macbeth persuades the murderers that they have every reason to hate Banquo. They reply that they are desperate men, willing to do anything.

87 **so gospelled**: such good Christians

89 **heavy ... grave**: ill-treatment has almost killed you

90 **beggared yours**: made beggars of your children
   Liege: lord / sovereign

91 **the catalogue**: i.e. the general list of living creatures

92–3 **curs ... demi-wolves**: kinds of dogs

93 **clept**: called

94 **file**: list putting them in order of value

95 **subtle**: clever

96 **housekeeper**: domestic watch-dog

97 **bounteous**: generous

98 **in him closed**: enclosed within him

99 **addition**: reputation

101 **station ... file**: place in the rank order

103 **put ... bosoms**: secretly reveal a plan to you

104 **takes ... off**: i.e. kills your enemy

105 **Grapples ... us**: makes you my closest friends

106–7 **Who ... perfect**: i.e. I am in a bad way while he is alive, but would feel perfect if he were dead

109 **so ... reckless**: so angered that I don't care

111 **tugged with**: knocked about by

112 **set ... chance**: take any gamble with my life

113 **mend**: improve

Think about

• What arguments does Macbeth use to persuade the murderers? What are the similarities and differences between these and the methods Lady Macbeth used on Macbeth himself in Act 1 Scene 7?

MACBETH	I did so – and went further, which is now	
	Our point of second meeting. Do you find	85
	Your patience so predominant in your nature	
	That you can let this go? Are you so gospelled	
	To pray for this good man, and for his issue,	
	Whose heavy hand hath bowed you to the grave	
	And beggared yours for ever?	

MURDERER 1   We are men, my Liege.   90

MACBETH   Ay, in the catalogue ye go for men –
             As hounds and greyhounds, mongrels, spaniels, curs,
             Shoughs, water-rugs, and demi-wolves are clept
             All by the name of dogs. The valued file
             Distinguishes the swift, the slow, the subtle,   95
             The housekeeper, the hunter, every one
             According to the gift which bounteous nature
             Hath in him closed – whereby he does receive
             Particular addition, from the bill
             That writes them all alike. And so of men.   100
             Now, if you have a station in the file,
             Not i' the worst rank of manhood, say it –
             And I will put that business in your bosoms,
             Whose execution takes your enemy off,
             Grapples you to the heart and love of us,   105
             Who wear our health but sickly in his life,
             Which in his death were perfect.

MURDERER 2   I am one, my Liege,
             Whom the vile blows and buffets of the world
             Have so incensed, that I am reckless what
             I do to spite the world.

MURDERER 1   And I another,   110
             So weary with disasters, tugged with fortune,
             That I would set my life on any chance
             To mend it or be rid on't.

MACBETH   Both of you
             Know Banquo was your enemy.

MURDERERS   True, my lord.

Macbeth explains to the murderers that it would be difficult for him simply to have Banquo executed because Banquo has too many friends. He commands the murderers to kill Banquo and his son Fleance that night.

115 **distance**: 1 hatred; 2 the space between two fencers

116–17 **thrusts ... life**: makes a stab at my heart

118 **With ... sight**: as King kill him openly

119 **bid ... it**: simply say that it was my decision

121 **loves ... drop**: support I cannot afford to lose

wail his fall: grieve over the death of a man

123 **to ... love**: ask for your help

124 **Masking ... eye**: hiding the affair from the public

125 **sundry weighty**: a variety of very good

127 **Your ... you**: i.e. I can see you're the right kind of men

129 **Acquaint ... time**: let you know the best opportunity for doing the murder

131 **something**: some distance

131–2 **always ... clearness**: and keeping in mind that I must remain free of suspicion

133 **rubs**: rough edges

botches: untidy work

135 **absence ... material**: death is no less important

137 **Resolve yourselves apart**: Go away and make up your minds

138 **anon**: immediately

139 **straight**: straight away

abide within: wait inside

Think about

• Why might Macbeth not want to kill Banquo himself?

• Why do you think the murderers do not question the need to kill Fleance as well as Banquo?

| MACBETH | So is he mine – and in such bloody distance | **115** |

MACBETH   So is he mine – and in such bloody distance   **115**
That every minute of his being thrusts
Against my near'st of life. And though I could
With bare-faced power sweep him from my sight,
And bid my will avouch it, yet I must not,
For certain friends, that are both his and mine,   **120**
Whose loves I may not drop, but wail his fall
Who I myself struck down. And thence it is
That I to your assistance do make love,
Masking the business from the common eye,
For sundry weighty reasons.

MURDERER 2   We shall, my lord,   **125**
Perform what you command us.

MURDERER 1   Though our lives –

MACBETH   Your spirits shine through you. Within this hour at most
I will advise you where to plant yourselves,
Acquaint you with the perfect spy o' the time,
The moment on't, for 't must be done tonight   **130**
And something from the palace; always thought
That I require a clearness. And with him
(To leave no rubs, nor botches, in the work),
Fleance his son, that keeps him company,
Whose absence is no less material to me   **135**
Than is his father's, must embrace the fate
Of that dark hour. Resolve yourselves apart:
I'll come to you anon.

MURDERER 2   We are resolved, my lord.

MACBETH   I'll call upon you straight: abide within. –

Exeunt MURDERERS.

It is concluded. Banquo, thy soul's flight,   **140**
If it find heaven, must find it out tonight.

Exit.

In this scene ...

- Though he is now King, Macbeth is worried about the dangers which still threaten him and Lady Macbeth.
- Refusing to tell Lady Macbeth about his plan to have Banquo killed, Macbeth concludes that evil deeds need to be backed up by further crimes.

Although Macbeth and Lady Macbeth have become King and Queen as they wanted, they are not happy. Lady Macbeth tells her husband that they cannot change what has happened. But Macbeth still fears those who could be a danger to them.

Think about

- What do the examples of antithesis (use of opposites) in lines 4 to 7 reveal about Lady Macbeth's state of mind?

- What are the differences between Lady Macbeth's and Macbeth's feelings about their current situation?

3–4 **attend ... words**: like a few words with him if it is convenient

4 **Nought's ... spent**: We have achieved nothing and have given everything
5 **Where ... content**: when we are not happy with what we have got
7 **by ... joy**: to kill and then have our happiness ruined by worries

9 **sorriest fancies**: depressing thoughts
11–12 **Things ... regard**: i.e. If you can't put something right, don't dwell on it
13 **scorched**: gashed / wounded
14 **close ... herself**: heal up
14–15 **poor ... Remains**: feeble attempts at violence leave us
15 **former tooth**: i.e. original venom
16 **frame ... disjoint**: universe fall apart
   both the worlds: i.e. heaven and earth
17 **Ere**: before
18 **affliction**: pain / torment

20 **to peace**: i.e. to heaven
22 **restless ecstasy**: sleepless madness
23 **fitful**: restless
24 **nor ... nor ...**: neither ... nor ...
25 **Malice ... levy**: trouble at home or foreign armies

ACT 3   SCENE 2

Forres: another room in the palace.

Enter LADY MACBETH, *with a* SERVANT.

LADY MACBETH	Is Banquo gone from court?
SERVANT	Ay, madam, but returns again tonight.
LADY MACBETH	Say to the King, I would attend his leisure For a few words.
SERVANT	Madam, I will.

Exit.

LADY MACBETH   Nought's had, all's spent,
Where our desire is got without content.   5
'Tis safer to be that which we destroy
Than by destruction dwell in doubtful joy.

Enter MACBETH.

How now, my lord? Why do you keep alone,
Of sorriest fancies your companions making,
Using those thoughts which should indeed have died   10
With them they think on? Things without all remedy
Should be without regard. What's done is done.

MACBETH   We have scorched the snake, not killed it:
She'll close and be herself – whilst our poor malice
Remains in danger of her former tooth.   15
But let the frame of things disjoint, both the worlds
        suffer,
Ere we will eat our meal in fear, and sleep
In the affliction of these terrible dreams
That shake us nightly. Better be with the dead
Whom we, to gain our peace, have sent to peace,   20
Than on the torture of the mind to lie
In restless ecstasy. Duncan is in his grave.
After life's fitful fever he sleeps well.
Treason has done his worst: nor steel, nor poison,
Malice domestic, foreign levy, nothing   25
Can touch him further.

Macbeth expresses his fears
about Banquo and Fleance, and
hints to Lady Macbeth that
something terrible is about to
happen to them.

27 **sleek o'er**: smooth over

30 **Let … apply**: Remember to pay special
attention
31 **Present him eminence**: Give him
special honour
32 **Unsafe the while**: the present time is
so unsafe
33 **lave our honours**: wash our
achievements
34 **vizards**: masks

38 **in … eterne**: their lives and bodies will
not last for ever
39 **assailable**: open to attack
40 **jocund**: cheerful
41 **cloistered**: 1 hidden; 2 through the
arches of old buildings
Hecate: the goddess of witchcraft
42 **shard-borne**: flying on scaly wings
43 **rung … peal**: i.e. the beetle's hum is
like the tolling of the evening bell,
rung when people are ready for bed
45 **chuck**: 'chick', a term of affection
46 **seeling**: blinding
47 **Scarf up**: blindfold
49 **Cancel … pieces**: i.e. Banquo's life is
like a legal document to be torn up
50 **pale**: 1 pale with fear; 2 'paled' /
fenced in
Light thickens: i.e. it becomes harder
to see
53 **black agents**: evil-doers
to … rouse: get up and hunt
55 **Things … ill**: Actions begun by evil are
reinforced by more evil
56 **prithee**: please

Think about

• Why doesn't Macbeth tell
Lady Macbeth what he is
planning to do? What does
this suggest about their
relationship at this point?
Think about how it is
different from their
relationship in Act 1.

LADY MACBETH	Come on,
	Gentle my lord: sleek o'er your rugged looks.
	Be bright and jovial among your guests tonight.

MACBETH	So shall I, love; and so, I pray, be you.	
	Let your remembrance apply to Banquo.	**30**
	Present him eminence, both with eye and tongue:	
	Unsafe the while, that we	
	Must lave our honours in these flattering streams,	
	And make our faces vizards to our hearts,	
	Disguising what they are.	

LADY MACBETH	You must leave this.	**35**

MACBETH	O, full of scorpions is my mind, dear wife!
	Thou know'st that Banquo and his Fleance lives.

LADY MACBETH	But in them nature's copy's not eterne.

MACBETH	There's comfort yet: they are assailable.	
	Then be thou jocund. Ere the bat hath flown	**40**
	His cloistered flight; ere to black Hecate's summons	
	The shard-borne beetle, with his drowsy hums,	
	Hath rung night's yawning peal, there shall be done	
	A deed of dreadful note.	

LADY MACBETH	What's to be done?

MACBETH	Be innocent of the knowledge, dearest chuck,	**45**
	Till thou applaud the deed. Come, seeling Night,	
	Scarf up the tender eye of pitiful day,	
	And, with thy bloody and invisible hand,	
	Cancel and tear to pieces that great bond	
	Which keeps me pale! - Light thickens; and the crow	**50**
	Makes wing to the rooky wood.	
	Good things of day begin to droop and drowse,	
	Whiles night's black agents to their preys do rouse.	
	Thou marvell'st at my words: but hold thee still.	
	Things bad begun make strong themselves by ill!	**55**
	So, prithee, go with me.	

Exeunt.

Act 3   Scene 3

In this scene ...

- A third man joins the two murderers sent to kill Banquo and Fleance.
- They are only partly successful; although they kill Banquo, Fleance escapes.

The two murderers whose job it is to kill Banquo and Fleance are joined by a third, sent by Macbeth. They hear Banquo and Fleance approaching.

2 He ... mistrust: We don't need to mistrust him

2–3 delivers our offices: tells us our duties

4 To ... just: i.e. exactly according to Macbeth's instructions

5 yet: still

6–7 spurs ... inn: the delayed traveller spurs his horse on to get to the inn on time

8 subject ... watch: man we are looking out for

10 within ... expectation: on the list of guests expected at the banquet

11 go about: are taking the long way round

Think about

- Who do you think the Third Murderer might be? Why might he have been sent to accompany the other two?
---

15 Stand to 't: Get ready

16 Let ... down: wordplay – applies to both the rain and their attack

Forres: a path near the palace.

Enter three MURDERERS.

MURDERER 1	But who did bid thee join with us?
MURDERER 3	Macbeth.
MURDERER 2	He needs not our mistrust, since he delivers Our offices, and what we have to do, To the direction just.

MURDERER 1   Then stand with us.
The west yet glimmers with some streaks of day: 5
Now spurs the lated traveller apace,
To gain the timely inn; and near approaches
The subject of our watch.

MURDERER 3   Hark! I hear horses.

BANQUO   (*Calling as he approaches*) Give us a light there, ho!

MURDERER 2   Then 'tis he. The rest
That are within the note of expectation   10
Already are i' the court.

MURDERER 1   His horses go about.

MURDERER 3   Almost a mile – but he does usually,
So all men do, from hence to the palace gate
Make it their walk.

Enter BANQUO, *and* FLEANCE *with a lighted torch.*

MURDERER 2   A light, a light!

MURDERER 3   'Tis he.

MURDERER 1   Stand to 't.   15

BANQUO   (*To* FLEANCE) It will be rain tonight.

MURDERER 1   Let it come down.

MURDERERS attack. FIRST MURDERER *strikes out Fleance's light.*

The murderers kill Banquo, but in the confusion Fleance manages to escape.

18 **may'st revenge**: will be able to get revenge for my death

19 **Was't ... way**: Wasn't that the right thing to do
20 **but one down**: only one killed

Think about

• Fleance manages to escape the three murderers. If you were the director, how would you make his escape seem realistic and believable?

• Why is it important in terms of the plot that Fleance should survive?

BANQUO   O, treachery! Fly, good Fleance! Fly, fly, fly!
Thou may'st revenge – O slave!

He is cut down and killed. FLEANCE *escapes.*

MURDERER 3   Who did strike out the light?

MURDERER 1   Was't not the way?

MURDERER 3   There's but one down. The son is fled.

MURDERER 2   We have lost   20
Best half of our affair.

MURDERER 1   Well, let's away, and say how much is done.

Exeunt.

In this scene ...

- Macbeth entertains the lords at a banquet. He is told by one of the murderers that Banquo is dead, but Fleance escaped.
- At the banquet, Macbeth sees Banquo's ghost. Despite Lady Macbeth's efforts to calm him, he cannot hide his terror, and the banquet ends abruptly.
- To find out more about the future, Macbeth decides to visit the Witches the following morning.

The banquet at Macbeth's castle begins. One of the murderers tells Macbeth in private that Banquo has been killed, but that Fleance escaped.

1 **degrees**: ranks / places
2 **at ... last**: i.e. a hearty welcome to one and all

3 **society**: the company

5 **keeps her state**: will remain seated
in best time: at an appropriate time

7 **Pronounce it**: i.e. Tell people how welcome they are

9 **encounter**: respond to

10 **Both ... even**: There are the same number of people on each side of the table
11 **Be ... mirth**: Enjoy yourselves
measure: toast

14 **'Tis ... within**: The blood is better on you than in him
15 **dispatched**: killed

19 **the nonpareil**: without equal

Think about

- What is significant about the frequency of the word 'welcome' and its position in each speech at the beginning of the scene? Look at lines 1 to 8.

Inside the palace. A table with a banquet is set out.

Enter MACBETH *and* LADY MACBETH, *with* ROSS *and* LENNOX,

other LORDS, *and attendants.* LADY MACBETH *takes her seat at*

one end of the table.

MACBETH	You know your own degrees, sit down: at first And last, The hearty welcome.
LORDS	Thanks to your Majesty.
MACBETH	Ourself will mingle with society, And play the humble host. Our hostess keeps her state, but in best time 5 We will require her welcome.
LADY MACBETH	Pronounce it for me, sir, to all our friends – For my heart speaks, they are welcome.

Enter FIRST MURDERER *(to the doorway).*

MACBETH	(*To* LADY MACBETH) See, they encounter thee with their
	    hearts' thanks.
	(*To all at the table*) Both sides are even: here I'll sit,
	    i' the midst. 10
	Be large in mirth. Anon, we'll drink a measure
	The table round. (*Moving to talk privately with the*
	    MURDERER *at the door*) There's blood upon thy face.

MURDERER	'Tis Banquo's then.
MACBETH	'Tis better thee without than he within. Is he dispatched? 15
MURDERER	My lord, his throat is cut: that I did for him.
MACBETH	Thou art the best o' the cut-throats. Yet he's good That did the like for Fleance: if thou didst it, Thou art the nonpareil.
MURDERER	Most royal Sir, Fleance is 'scaped. 20

Macbeth is dismayed by the
news that Fleance escaped. But
he returns to the banquet and
pretends to be disappointed at
Banquo's absence from the
meal. The ghost of Banquo
appears in Macbeth's seat at the
table.

21 **fit**: fit of anxiety
   else: otherwise
22 **Whole ... marble**: i.e. solid as marble
   founded: secure
23 **As ... air**: as free and unrestrained as
   the air which surrounds us
24 **cabined, cribbed**: closed in, restricted
25 **saucy**: nagging
   safe: dealt with
26 **bides**: remains
27 **trenchèd**: cut deep like trenches
28 **The ... nature**: the smallest of which
   would have been enough to kill him
29 **grown serpent**: i.e. Banquo
   worm: i.e. Fleance
31 **No ... present**: i.e. Fleance is harmless
   for the time being
32 **hear ourselves**: discuss this

33 **give the cheer**: behave like a good host
33–5 **The feast ... welcome**: If you don't
   keep telling people that they are
   welcome, they feel as though they
   have paid for their meal
35 **To feed ... home**: They might as well
   stay at home if they just want to eat
36 **From ... ceremony**: away from home,
   it is courteous behaviour by the host
   that makes a meal special
37 **Sweet remembrancer**: i.e. Thanks for
   reminding me, my love
40 **country's honour**: greatest nobles
   roofed: under one roof
42 **unkindness**: bad manners
43 **mischance**: an accident
44 **Lays ... promise**: suggests he has
   broken his promise

Think about

• What does Macbeth's
language (lines 21 to 25)
suggest about his state of
mind? Look at his use of
similes in lines 22 and 23,
and the contrasting
language of 24 to 25.

• How would you represent
Banquo's ghost in (a) a
stage version; and (b) a
film? Should the ghost be
visible to the audience or
not, in your opinion?

MACBETH	(*Aside*) Then comes my fit again. I had else been	
	perfect –	
	Whole as the marble, founded as the rock,	
	As broad and general as the casing air:	
	But now I am cabined, cribbed, confined, bound in	
	To saucy doubts and fears. – (*To the* MURDERER) But	
	Banquo's safe?	25

MURDERER   Ay, my good lord. Safe in a ditch he bides,
With twenty trenchèd gashes on his head –
The least a death to nature.

MACBETH   Thanks for that. –
(*Aside*) There the grown serpent lies: the worm, that's
    fled,
Hath nature that in time will venom breed –   30
No teeth for the present. – (*To the* MURDERER) Get
    thee gone. Tomorrow
We'll hear ourselves again.

                                   Exit MURDERER.

LADY MACBETH   My royal lord,
You do not give the cheer. The feast is sold
That is not often vouched, while 'tis a-making,
'Tis given with welcome. To feed were best at home: 35
From thence, the sauce to meat is ceremony.
Meeting were bare without it.

MACBETH   Sweet remembrancer! –
Now, good digestion wait on appetite,
And health on both!

LENNOX   May it please your Highness sit?

MACBETH   Here had we now our country's honour roofed,   40
Were the graced person of our Banquo present –

Enter the GHOST OF BANQUO. *It takes Macbeth's seat at the table.*

Who may I rather challenge for unkindness,
Than pity for mischance!

ROSS   His absence, sir,
Lays blame upon his promise. Please 't your Highness
To grace us with your royal company?   45

Macbeth is terrified by the sight of Banquo's ghost in his seat. Lady Macbeth tries to reassure the lords, who cannot see the ghost, that her husband's strange behaviour is nothing to worry about. She privately speaks sharply to Macbeth for revealing his fear.

51 **gory locks**: bloody hair

53 **thus**: like this

55 **upon a thought**: in a moment
56 **much … him**: you stare at him
57 **extend his passion**: prolong the fit

60 **O proper stuff**: Nonsense
61 **This … fear**: Your fear is causing you to imagine this
63 **flaws and starts**: sudden outbursts of emotion
64 **Impostors to**: false compared with
   become: suit
66 **Authorised … grandam**: true according to her grandmother

69 **Prithee**: I beg you

71 **charnel-houses**: bone-stores
73 **maws**: stomachs
   kites: birds that feed off the flesh of dead animals

Think about

• Why does nobody except Macbeth see the ghost?

• What similarities can you see between Lady Macbeth's language here and her methods of persuasion in Act 1 Scene 7?

MACBETH	The table's full.
LENNOX	Here is a place reserved, sir.
MACBETH	Where?
LENNOX	Here, my good lord. (MACBETH *sees the* GHOST.) What is't that moves your Highness?
MACBETH	Which of you have done this?
LORDS	What, my good lord?
MACBETH	(*To the* GHOST) Thou canst not say I did it! Never shake 50 Thy gory locks at me!
ROSS	Gentlemen, rise: his Highness is not well.
LADY MACBETH	Sit, worthy friends. My lord is often thus, And hath been from his youth. Pray you, keep seat. The fit is momentary: upon a thought 55 He will again be well. If much you note him You shall offend him, and extend his passion. (*Rising from the table*) Feed, and regard him not. – (*Aside to* MACBETH) Are you a man?
MACBETH	Ay, and a bold one, that dare look on that Which might appal the devil.
LADY MACBETH	O proper stuff! 60 This is the very painting of your fear: This is the air-drawn dagger which, you said, Led you to Duncan. O! – these flaws and starts (Impostors to true fear) would well become A woman's story at a winter's fire, 65 Authorised by her grandam. Shame itself! Why do you make such faces? When all's done, You look but on a stool.
MACBETH	Prithee, see there! Behold! Look! Lo! – how say you? Why – what care I? (*To the* GHOST) If thou canst nod, speak too! – 70 If charnel-houses and our graves must send Those that we bury back, our monuments Shall be the maws of kites!

Exit GHOST.

Macbeth apologises to the lords and tries to regain his calmness, but is again terrified when the ghost reappears.

73 **Quite ... folly**: Has your foolishness made you lose your manhood completely

75 **ere**: before
76 **humane ... weal**: human laws cleansed society and made it civilised

79 **when ... out**: when a man had had his brains bashed out
81 **mortal ... crowns**: fatal wounds on their heads

84 **do lack you**: are missing your company

85 **muse**: be surprised
86 **infirmity**: weakness

Think about

- What is it about the appearance and behaviour of Banquo's ghost that Macbeth finds particularly terrifying? Look at Macbeth's reaction in lines 49 to 51, 69 to 73, 75 to 83, and 93 to 96.

- What do you think the Lords are making of Macbeth's behaviour and the reason he gives for it? Look at lines 84 to 87.

---

92 **all to all**: Good health to everyone

pledge: toast
93 **Avaunt**: Be gone

95 **Thou ... eyes**: there is no sign of life in your eyes

97 **a thing of custom**: nothing out of the ordinary

LADY MACBETH	What! Quite unmanned in folly?
MACBETH	If I stand here, I saw him!
LADY MACBETH	Fie! – for shame!

MACBETH Blood hath been shed ere now, i' the olden time,   75
Ere humane statute purged the gentle weal –
Ay, and since too, murders have been performed
Too terrible for the ear. The time has been
That, when the brains were out, the man would die,
And there an end. But now they rise again   80
With twenty mortal murders on their crowns,
And push us from our stools. This is more strange
Than such a murder is.

LADY MACBETH   My worthy lord,
Your noble friends do lack you.

MACBETH   I do forget. –
(*To the* LORDS) Do not muse at me, my most worthy
    friends.   85
I have a strange infirmity, which is nothing
To those that know me. Come, love and health to all.
Then I'll sit down. – Give me some wine: fill full. –
I drink to the general joy o' the whole table –
And to our dear friend Banquo, whom we miss.   90
Would he were here.

Re-enter the GHOST.

To all, and him, we thirst –
And all to all.

LORDS   Our duties – and the pledge.

MACBETH (*To the* GHOST) Avaunt and quit my sight! Let the earth
    hide thee!
Thy bones are marrowless, thy blood is cold –
Thou hast no speculation in those eyes   95
Which thou dost glare with!

LADY MACBETH   (*To the* LORDS) Think of this, good peers,
But as a thing of custom: 'tis no other –
Only it spoils the pleasure of the time.

Unable to control her husband's strange behaviour, Lady Macbeth eventually tells the lords to leave.

101 **Hyrcan**: from Hyrcania, wild country by the Caspian Sea
102 **but *that***: i.e. except Banquo's
104 **dare … desert**: i.e. to a fight to the death, with no-one around to interrupt
105–6 **If … girl**: If I fear and tremble then, you can call me a feeble creature

109 **displaced the mirth**: ruined the good mood of the feast
110 **most admired disorder**: this amazing fit of madness

112–6 **You … fear**: i.e. I always thought I was brave; but I am amazed to see you unmoved by such sights

116 **blanched**: turned white

119 **Stand … going**: Don't worry about leaving in order of rank

122 **It will … blood**: i.e. murder will lead to more bloodshed or execution

Think about

• Order and disorder are important in this play. How is disorder represented in this part of the scene? Look at Lady Macbeth's speeches in lines 109 to 110, and 117 to 120.

• Lady Macbeth has taunted Macbeth with being 'unmanned' (line 73). What seems to be their definition of 'manhood'? Look, for example, at lines 99 to 106, and 112 to 116.

MACBETH	What man dare, I dare!
	Approach thou like the rugged Russian bear, **100**
	The armed rhinoceros, or the Hyrcan tiger –
	Take any shape but *that*, and my firm nerves
	Shall never tremble. Or be alive again,
	And dare me to the desert with thy sword –
	If trembling I inhabit then, protest me **105**
	The baby of a girl! Hence horrible shadow! –
	Unreal mockery! Hence! –

Exit GHOST.

	Why, so. – Being gone,
	I am a man again. – (*To the* LORDS) Pray you, sit still.
LADY MACBETH	(*To* MACBETH) You have displaced the mirth, broke
	the good meeting,
	With most admired disorder.
MACBETH	Can such things be, **110**
	And overcome us like a summer's cloud,
	Without our special wonder? You make me strange
	Even to the disposition that I owe,
	When now I think you can behold such sights
	And keep the natural ruby of your cheeks, **115**
	When mine is blanched with fear.
ROSS	What sights, my lord?
LADY MACBETH	(*To the* LORDS) I pray you, speak not: he grows worse
	and worse.
	Question enrages him. At once, good night. –
	Stand not upon the order of your going,
	But go at once.
LENNOX	Good night, and better health **120**
	Attend his Majesty!
LADY MACBETH	A kind good night to all.

Exit LENNOX, *with* ROSS, *other* LORDS *and attendants.*

MACBETH	It will have blood, they say, blood will have blood.

Macbeth thinks about the many ways in which murders come to light. He finds it suspicious that Macduff refused to attend that night's banquet and decides to visit the Witches again the next morning. He now knows that he will have to commit further bloody deeds.

Think about

- What does Macbeth say which shows that he is (a) superstitious; (b) suspicious of his lords; and (c) prepared to commit more violence? Look at lines 122 onwards.

- What is the significance of line 141? What does it recall from earlier in the play?

124 **Augurs … relations**: Prophecies and knowledge about how events are linked

125 **maggot-pies … rooks**: birds used as omens

125–6 **brought … blood**: exposed the most hidden murderers

127 **Almost … which**: i.e. Night is arguing with morning about which it is

128 **denies his person**: refuses to be present

130 **by the way**: on the grapevine

132 **fee'd**: paid by me (as a spy)

133 **betimes**: very early

134 **bent**: determined

135 **the worst means**: the most evil methods (i.e. witchcraft)

135–6 **For mine … way**: I will sacrifice everything else to get what I want

138 **go o'er**: crossing to the other side

139 **will to hand**: must be put into practice

140 **acted … scanned**: i.e. acted upon before I think too much about them

141 **season**: preservative, i.e. what keeps us fresh

142 **self-abuse**: self-deception (imagining Banquo's ghost)

143 **initiate**: beginner's

144 **young in deed**: i.e. new to crimes like this

Stones have been known to move, and trees to speak.
Augurs, and understood relations, have
By maggot-pies and choughs, and rooks, brought forth   **125**
The secret'st man of blood. What is the night?

LADY MACBETH   Almost at odds with morning, which is which.

MACBETH   How say'st thou, that Macduff denies his person
At our great bidding?

LADY MACBETH   Did you send to him, sir?

MACBETH   I hear it by the way: but I will send.   **130**
There's not a one of them, but in his house
I keep a servant fee'd. I will tomorrow –
And betimes I will – to the weird sisters.
More shall they speak – for now I am bent to know
By the worst means, the worst. For mine own good   **135**
All causes shall give way. I am in blood
Stepped in so far, that, should I wade no more,
Returning were as tedious as go o'er.
Strange things I have in head, that will to hand,
Which must be acted ere they may be scanned.   **140**

LADY MACBETH   You lack the season of all natures, sleep.

MACBETH   Come, we'll to sleep. My strange and self-abuse
Is the initiate fear, that wants hard use.
We are yet but young in deed.

Exeunt.

Ludlow Festival, 2001

RSC, 1993

National Theatre, 1972

RSC, 1982

Act 3 Scene 5

In this scene ...

- The Witches are visited by the Witch goddess Hecate, who is angry about the way they have dealt with Macbeth.

The Witch goddess Hecate is angry that the Witches have not involved her in their dealings with Macbeth. She vows to lead Macbeth to his destruction.

Think about

- What does Hecate's speech lead us to believe about (a) the Witches' power and its limitations; and (b) what Macbeth's ultimate fate will be?

2 **beldams**: hags
3 **Saucy**: impertinent
4 **traffic**: have dealings

7 **close contriver**: secret plotter
8 **bear my part**: take part

11 **wayward son**: unreliable follower
12 **wrathful**: angry
13 **Loves ... ends**: loves witchcraft purely for what he can get out of it
15 **Acheron**: One of the rivers of the underworld, in classical mythology.
16 **Thither**: There
21 **Unto ... end**: planning something ruinous and deadly
24 **vaporous drop**: People believed that the moon shed drops of powerful foam onto certain plants which could then be used in witches' spells.
profound: ready to fall
26 **distilled**: i.e. turned into something powerful
sleights: tricks
27 **artificial sprites**: spirits raised by magic
28 **illusion**: power to deceive
29 **confusion**: destruction
30 **spurn**: think nothing of
30–1 **bear ... 'bove**: have unrealistic hopes and be blind to
32 **security**: over-confidence
33 **mortals**: i.e. ordinary humans

Thunder.

Enter the three Witches*, meeting* Hecate *(the Witch goddess).*

Witch 1   Why, how now, Hecate? You look angerly.

Hecate   Have I not reason, beldams as you are,
Saucy, and overbold? How did you dare
To trade and traffic with Macbeth,
In riddles, and affairs of death?   5
And I, the mistress of your charms,
The close contriver of all harms,
Was never called to bear my part,
Or show the glory of our art?
And, which is worse, all you have done   10
Hath been but for a wayward son,
Spiteful and wrathful – who, as others do,
Loves for his own ends, not for you.
But make amends now. Get you gone,
And at the pit of Acheron   15
Meet me i' the morning. Thither he
Will come to know his destiny.
Your vessels and your spells provide,
Your charms, and everything beside.
I am for the air. This night I'll spend   20
Unto a dismal and a fatal end.
Great business must be wrought ere noon.
Upon the corner of the moon
There hangs a vaporous drop profound.
I'll catch it ere it come to ground –   25
And that, distilled by magic sleights,
Shall raise such artificial sprites,
As, by the strength of their illusion,
Shall draw him on to his confusion.
He shall spurn fate, scorn death, and bear   30
His hopes 'bove wisdom, grace and fear.
And you all know, security
Is mortals' chiefest enemy.

Hecate is called away.

35 **stays**: waits

—Think about—————

• This scene is often cut in
  performance. Why might
  some directors decide to
  cut it?

• If it is included, what does
  it add in terms of (a) the
  plot; (b) the supernatural
  atmosphere; (c) our
  understanding of Macbeth;
  and (d) our understanding
  of the Witches and their
  motives?

Music and singing heard in the distance ('Come away, come away, Hecate, Hecate, come away! ...').

Hark! I am called. My little spirit, see,
Sits in a foggy cloud, and stays for me.   35

Exit.

WITCH 1   Come, let's make haste! She'll soon be back again.

Exeunt.

Act 3 Scene 6

In this scene ...

- Lennox talks about Macbeth's murderous behaviour with another lord.
- The lord tells Lennox that Malcolm has fled to England and that Macduff has gone there to seek support for an attempt to overthrow Macbeth.

Lennox tells another lord that he is suspicious about the deaths of Duncan and Banquo. The lord reports that Malcolm is with the English King, Edward the Confessor, and that Macduff has gone there hoping to find support for an attack on Macbeth.

Think about

- In what tone should an actor playing Lennox speak lines 3 to 20? Think about the difference between what he says and what he really means.

1 **My former speeches**: What I have already said
but ... thoughts: simply matches what you have been thinking
2 **Which ... farther**: it's up to you to draw your own conclusions
3 **Things ... borne**: mysterious things have happened
4 **of**: by
8 **want the thought**: help thinking
10 **fact**: crime
11 **straight**: straightaway
12 **pious**: loyal
delinquents: i.e. Duncan's two attendants
13 **thralls**: prisoners
17 **borne**: managed
18 **under his key**: in prison
19 **an't**: if it

21 **from broad words**: because of his outspoken comments
22 **tyrant**: i.e. Macbeth
24 **bestows himself**: is staying
25 **due of birth**: i.e. crown which is rightfully his
28 **malevolence of fortune**: i.e. loss of Malcolm's throne
28–9 **nothing ... respect**: has not meant that he has received less respect
29 **Thither**: There, i.e. to England
30 **pray**: ask
upon his aid: on Malcolm's behalf
31 **wake**: rouse up

132

Forres: the edge of the town.

Enter Lennox, *with another* Lord.

LENNOX   My former speeches have but hit your thoughts,
         Which can interpret farther. Only, I say,
         Things have been strangely borne. The gracious
             Duncan
         Was pitied of Macbeth. Marry, he was dead.
         And the right-valiant Banquo walked too late –   5
         Whom you may say, if 't please you, Fleance killed,
         For Fleance fled. Men must not walk too late.
         Who cannot want the thought how monstrous
         It was for Malcolm and for Donalbain
         To kill their gracious father? Damnèd fact!   10
         How it did grieve Macbeth! Did he not straight,
         In pious rage, the two delinquents tear,
         That were the slaves of drink, and thralls of sleep?
         Was not that nobly done? Ay, and wisely, too.
         For 'twould have angered any heart alive   15
         To hear the men deny 't. So that, I say,
         He has borne all things well. And I do think
         That, had he Duncan's sons under his key –
         As, an't please Heaven, he shall not – they should find
         What 'twere to kill a father. So should Fleance.   20
         But, peace! – For from broad words, and 'cause he
             failed
         His presence at the tyrant's feast, I hear
         Macduff lives in disgrace. Sir, can you tell
         Where he bestows himself?

LORD   The son of Duncan,
         From whom this tyrant holds the due of birth,   25
         Lives in the English court – and is received
         Of the most pious Edward with such grace,
         That the malevolence of fortune nothing
         Takes from his high respect. Thither Macduff
         Is gone to pray the holy King, upon his aid,   30
         To wake Northumberland, and warlike Siward –

Lennox and the lord agree that
Macduff would be well advised
to stay out of Macbeth's way.

32 Him above: God
33 ratify: support

36 Do … honours: show our loyal duty to
the King and be honestly rewarded
37 pine: painfully long
38 exasperate: angered

41 cloudy: scowling (at Macduff's refusal
to submit)
42–3 rue … answer: come to regret that you
answered me like this
44 Advise … caution: warn Macduff to be
careful
44–5 hold … provide: keep a sensible
distance from Macbeth

49 accursed: i.e. wicked

---Think about---

• What are the main
purposes of this scene in
performance – apart from
giving the actor playing
Macbeth a rest? Think about
what information it
conveys, which new
characters who might
become important later are
referred to, and what it tells
us about the situation in
Scotland.

• Look at the final speeches
by Lennox and the lord
(lines 45 to 49). How does
the language reflect their
feelings that the forces
against Macbeth are holy,
while Macbeth himself is
damned?

That, by the help of these (with Him above
To ratify the work), we may again
Give to our tables meat, sleep to our nights,
Free from our feasts and banquets bloody knives,   35
Do faithful homage, and receive free honours –
All which we pine for now. And this report
Hath so exasperate the King that he
Prepares for some attempt of war.

LENNOX   Sent he to Macduff?

LORD He did. And with an absolute 'Sir, not I,'   40
The cloudy messenger turns me his back,
And hums, as who should say, 'You'll rue the time
That clogs me with this answer.'

LENNOX   And that well might
Advise him to a caution, to hold what distance
His wisdom can provide. Some holy angel   45
Fly to the court of England and unfold
His message ere he come – that a swift blessing
May soon return to this our suffering country
Under a hand accursed!

LORD   I'll send my prayers with him.

Exeunt.

Act 4 Scene 1

In this scene ...

- Macbeth visits the Witches and is shown a series of mysterious visions about what will happen in the future.
- As the Witches disappear, Lennox arrives to report that Macduff has gone to England.
- Macbeth instantly decides to kill everyone in Macduff's castle.

The Witches prepare for their meeting with Macbeth by creating a powerful magic potion.

Think about

- What would be an effective setting for this scene (a) on stage; and (b) in a film?

- The Witches use 'Liver of blaspheming Jew' (line 26). In Shakespeare's time there was an irrational hatred of Jews who were wrongly blamed for Christ's death. If you were a director, how would you reply to an actor who said 'I'm not saying that line – it's racist'?

1 **brindled**: tabby

2 **hedge-pig**: hedgehog

3 **Harpier**: the third Witch's attendant spirit

5 **entrails**: animals' insides

8 **Sweltered venom**: has been sweating out poison
sleeping got: taken while sleeping

12 **Fillet**: A thin slice
fenny: found in bogs and marshes

16 **fork**: forked tongue
blind-worm: slow-worm (a harmless snake-like lizard)

17 **howlet**: young owl

23 **Witches' mummy**: a medicinal powder made from Egyptian mummies
maw and gulf: stomach and throat

24 **ravined ... shark**: a shark that has eaten its fill

25 **hemlock**: a poisonous plant

26 **blaspheming**: speaking against God

27 **Gall**: bitter fluid from the liver
slips: cuttings

28 **Slivered**: sliced off

29–30 **Turk ... Tartar ... birth-strangled babe**: Like the Jew, all would be attractive to the Witches because they were not christened.

ACT 4   SCENE 1

A shadowy cavern: a steaming cauldron at its centre.

Thunder.

Enter the three WITCHES.

WITCH 1	Thrice the brindled cat hath mewed.
WITCH 2	Thrice and once the hedge-pig whined.
WITCH 3	Harpier cries – 'tis time, 'tis time!

WITCH 1   Round about the cauldron go –
In the poisoned entrails throw.   5
Toad, that under cold stone
Days and nights has thirty-one
Sweltered venom, sleeping got,
Boil thou first i' the charmèd pot.

ALL   Double, double, toil and trouble –   10
Fire burn and cauldron bubble!

WITCH 2   Fillet of a fenny snake,
In the cauldron boil and bake –
Eye of newt, and toe of frog,
Wool of bat and tongue of dog,   15
Adder's fork, and blind-worm's sting,
Lizard's leg, and howlet's wing –
For a charm of powerful trouble,
Like a hell-broth boil and bubble.

ALL   Double, double, toil and trouble –   20
Fire burn and cauldron bubble!

WITCH 3   Scale of dragon, tooth of wolf,
Witches' mummy, maw and gulf
Of the ravined salt-sea shark,
Root of hemlock digged i' the dark;   25
Liver of blaspheming Jew,
Gall of goat, and slips of yew
Slivered in the moon's eclipse;
Nose of Turk, and Tartar's lips;

Hecate enters with three more Witches. Macbeth arrives and commands the Witches to answer his questions, whatever the consequences.

31 **drab**: prostitute
32 **slab**: sticky
33 **chawdron**: insides

39 **commend your pains**: congratulate you on your efforts

44 **pricking ... thumbs**: People believed that sudden pains were a sign that something was about to happen.

Think about

- Which speech here picks up the important theme of disorder? What form does the disorder take?

- Look at the form of verse in which the Witches speak here and find examples of internal rhyme and a four-beat rhythm. Why is this sort of verse suited to the uttering of spells?

---

50 **conjure**: call upon
   profess: practise, i.e. witchcraft
52–3 **untie ... churches**: i.e. cause the wind to knock churches down
53 **yeasty**: foaming
54 **Confound ... up**: confuse and overwhelm ships
55 **bladed ... lodged**: unripe corn be blown flat
57 **slope**: bend / collapse

	Finger of birth-strangled babe,	30
	Ditch-delivered by a drab –	
	Make the gruel thick and slab.	
	Add thereto a tiger's chawdron,	
	For th' ingredients of our cauldron.	

ALL Double, double, toil and trouble –   35
Fire burn and cauldron bubble!

WITCH 2 Cool it with a baboon's blood –
Then the charm is firm and good.

Enter HECATE, *with three more Witches.*

HECATE O well done! I commend your pains,
And every one shall share i' the gains.   40
And now about the cauldron sing,
Like elves and fairies in a ring,
Enchanting all that you put in.

Music. All the WITCHES *join in a wild dance round the cauldron
and sing – 'Black spirits and white, red spirits and grey, Mingle,
mingle ...'.*

Exit HECATE, *with the Witches who came with her.*

WITCH 2 By the pricking of my thumbs
Something wicked this way comes! –   45
Open, locks –
Whoever knocks.

Enter MACBETH.

MACBETH How now, you secret, black and midnight hags!
What is't you do?

ALL   A deed without a name.

MACBETH I conjure you by that which you profess,   50
Howe'er you come to know it, answer me.
Though you untie the winds and let them fight
Against the churches, though the yeasty waves
Confound and swallow navigation up –
Though bladed corn be lodged and trees blown down,   55
Though castles topple on their warders' heads,
Though palaces and pyramids do slope

The Witches summon apparitions to give Macbeth the answers he wants. An armoured head warns Macbeth to beware of Macduff. Next a blood-stained child appears.

59 **nature's germens**: the seeds of creation
60 **sicken**: i.e. is sick (with over-eating)

63 **our masters**: the spirits that the Witches serve

65 **nine farrow**: litter of nine piglets
65–6 **Grease … gibbet**: Sweat, that's dripped from a murderer who has been hanged

68 **office**: your function (to appear and foretell what will happen)
    deftly: skilfully

Think about

• There is some argument about what the 'armoured head' represents. Some people think that it is Macbeth's own head, cut off by Macduff; others that it is Macduff himself. What do you think? Could it represent anything else?

74 **harped**: guessed
    aright: correctly

76 **potent**: powerful

s.d. **a bloodstained child**: representing Macduff, 'untimely ripped' from his mother's womb (see Act 5 Scene 8, lines 15 to 16)

Their heads to their foundations – though the treasure
Of nature's germens tumble all together
Even till destruction sicken! – answer me   60
To what I ask you.

WITCH 1   Speak.

WITCH 2   Demand.

WITCH 3   We'll answer.

WITCH 1   Say, if thou'dst rather hear it from our mouths,
Or from our masters.

MACBETH   Call 'em. Let me see 'em.

WITCH 1   Pour in sow's blood, that hath eaten
Her nine farrow. Grease, that's sweaten   65
From the murderer's gibbet, throw
Into the flame.

ALL   Come, high or low! –
Thyself and office deftly show.

Thunder,
First APPARITION *– an armoured head – rises above the cauldron.*

MACBETH   Tell me, thou unknown power, –

WITCH 1   He knows thy thought.
Hear his speech, but say thou nought.   70

APPARITION 1   Macbeth! Macbeth! Macbeth! Beware Macduff!
Beware the Thane of Fife! Dismiss me. – Enough.

                              APPARITION *sinks from sight.*

MACBETH   Whate'er thou art, for thy good caution, thanks:
Thou hast harped my fear aright. But one word more –

WITCH 1   He will not be commanded. Here's another,   75
More potent than the first.

Thunder.
Second APPARITION *– a bloodstained child – rises.*

APPARITION 2   Macbeth! Macbeth! Macbeth! –

MACBETH   Had I three ears, I'd hear thee!

The second apparition tells Macbeth that he can't be harmed by a man born of a woman. Despite this reassurance, Macbeth vows to kill Macduff. A third apparition tells Macbeth that he cannot be defeated until Birnam Wood comes to his castle. Macbeth then asks whether Banquo's descendants will ever be kings of Scotland.

Think about

- Think about what each of the three apparitions might represent. Why do you think the Witches are showing them to Macbeth? To help him? To lead him to destruction?

- How would you describe Macbeth's attitude to the apparitions? Why do you think he responds in this way?

80 **none … born**: no man that a woman has given birth to

83 **make … sure**: make doubly sure (by killing Macduff anyway, even though he supposedly cannot be harmed by him)
84 **take … fate**: i.e. make Fate stick to its contract
s.d. **a child … hand**: representing Malcolm, the true King, with a tree from Birnam Wood (see Act 5 Scene 4, lines 4 to 7)
87 **issue**: descendant / child
88–9 **round … sovereignty**: i.e. the crown

90 **lion-mettled**: courageous as a lion
91 **chafes**: is angry
   frets: complains
92 **vanquished**: defeated

95 **impress the forest**: make the forest join an army
96 **bodements**: predictions
97 **Rebellious dead**: Those who have been killed for opposing Macbeth
99 **lease of nature**: full natural life-span
99–100 **pay … custom**: die in the normal way (as if paying a debt)
101 **art**: skill (of witchcraft)

APPARITION 2   Be bloody, bold and resolute! Laugh to scorn
The power of man – for none of woman born   80
Shall harm Macbeth.

                                 APPARITION *sinks away.*

MACBETH   Then live, Macduff. What need I fear of thee?
But yet I'll make assurance double sure,
And take a bond of fate: thou shalt not live! –
That I may tell pale-hearted fear it lies,   85
And sleep in spite of thunder. –

Thunder.
Third APPARITION *– a child wearing a crown, with a small*
green tree in his hand – rises.

                                      What is this,
That rises like the issue of a king,
And wears upon his baby brow the round
And top of sovereignty?

ALL   Listen – but speak not to it.

APPARITION 3   Be lion-mettled, proud, and take no care   90
Who chafes, who frets, or where conspirers are!
Macbeth shall never vanquished be, until
Great Birnam wood to high Dunsinane hill
Shall come against him.

                                 APPARITION *sinks away.*

MACBETH   That will never be!
Who can impress the forest? Bid the tree   95
Unfix his earth-bound root? Sweet bodements! Good!
Rebellious dead, rise never, till the wood
Of Birnam rise – and our high-placed Macbeth
Shall live the lease of nature, pay his breath
To time and mortal custom. – Yet my heart   100
Throbs to know one thing. Tell me (if your art
Can tell so much), shall Banquo's issue ever
Reign in this kingdom?

ALL   Seek to know no more.

MACBETH   I will be satisfied! Deny me this,
And an eternal curse fall on you! Let me know. –   105

The Witches show Macbeth a procession of eight Kings, accompanied by the ghost of Banquo himself. Macbeth is shocked to realise that the Kings are Banquo's descendants.

s.d. **a procession ... mirror**: a silent procession of eight Kings, descended from Banquo, who are also the ancestors of James I

113 **sear**: scorch

116 **Start**: Jump from your sockets
crack of doom: dawning of the day of Judgement

119 **glass**: mirror

121 **two-fold ... sceptres**: These represent the orbs carried in the double coronation of King James in Scotland and England; the treble sceptres are the two used in the English coronation and one in the Scottish.

123 **blood-boltered**: with hair clotted with blood

124 **for his**: claiming them as his descendants

127 **sprites**: spirits

130 **antic round**: i.e. a strange, grotesque dance

132 **Our ... pay**: we treated him well and made it worth his while coming here

Think about

• How would you represent the three apparitions and the show of Kings (a) on stage; and (b) in a film?

• What are the advantages and disadvantages of having the Witches played by men, as they would have been in Shakespeare's time and sometimes are now?

Eerie music (oboes): the Witches' cauldron begins to sink away.

Why sinks that cauldron? And what noise is this?

WITCH 1   Show!

WITCH 2   Show!

WITCH 3   Show!

ALL   Show his eyes, and grieve his heart!   110
Come like shadows – so depart.

*Enter a procession of eight phantom KINGS, the last of them
carrying a mirror. The GHOST of BANQUO follows them.*

MACBETH   (*To the first KING*) Thou art too like the spirit of
    Banquo! Down!
Thy crown does sear mine eye-balls! (*To the second*)
    And thy hair,
Thou other gold-bound brow, is like the first.
A third is like the former. – Filthy hags! –   115
Why do you show me this? – A fourth? – Start, eyes!
What! – Will the line stretch out t' the crack of doom?
Another yet? – A seventh? – I'll see no more! –
And yet the eighth appears, who bears a glass
Which shows me many more. And some I see   120
That two-fold balls and treble sceptres carry.
Horrible sight! – Now, I see 'tis true –
For the blood-boltered Banquo smiles upon me,
And points at them for his. – What! Is this so?

WITCH 1   Ay, sir, all this is so.

Phantom KINGS and GHOST disappear.

    – But why   125
Stands Macbeth thus amazèdly?
Come, sisters, cheer we up his sprites,
And show the best of our delights.
I'll charm the air to give a sound,
While you perform your antic round –   130
That this great King may kindly say,
Our duties did his welcome pay.

The Witches vanish. Lennox arrives to report that Macduff has fled to England. Macbeth decides to attack Macduff's castle and to kill his family.

133 **pernicious**: harmful
134 **Stand aye accursèd**: be forever cursed
135 **without there**: you outside

144 **thou … exploits**: you are one step ahead of my terrible actions
145–6 **The flighty … it**: i.e. unless you perform a deed the moment you think of it, it is too late
147–8 **The very … hand**: I will act as soon as I think
149 **crown my thoughts**: round off
150 **surprise**: attack suddenly
151 **give … sword:** i.e. kill
153 **That … line**: i.e. his descendants
154 **before … cool**: while I am still fired up to do it

Think about

- How far do you think each of these adjectives describes Macbeth at this point in the play: courageous, impulsive, violent, cowardly, superstitious, intelligent, deceitful, practical, and frightened?

- How do you react to Macbeth's resolution and his next plan of action (lines 146 to 154)?

Music. The WITCHES *circle in a wild dance, then vanish.*

MACBETH   Where are they? Gone? – Let this pernicious hour
Stand aye accursèd in the calendar! –
Come in, without there!

Enter LENNOX.

LENNOX   What's your Grace's will?   135

MACBETH   Saw you the weird sisters?

LENNOX   No, my lord.

MACBETH   Came they not by you?

LENNOX   No, indeed, my lord.

MACBETH   Infected be the air whereon they ride –
And damned all those that trust them! – I did hear
The galloping of horse. Who was't came by?   140

LENNOX   'Tis two or three, my lord, that bring you word
Macduff is fled to England.

MACBETH   Fled to England?

LENNOX   Ay, my good lord.

MACBETH   (*Aside*) Time, thou anticipat'st my dread exploits:
The flighty purpose never is o'ertook,   145
Unless the deed go with it. From this moment
The very firstlings of my heart shall be
The firstlings of my hand. And even now,
To crown my thoughts with acts, be it thought and
    done.
The castle of Macduff I will surprise: 150
Seize upon Fife – give to the edge o' the sword
His wife, his babes, and all unfortunate souls
That trace him in his line. No boasting, like a fool –
This deed I'll do before this purpose cool!
But no more sights! – (*To* LENNOX) Where are these
    gentlemen?   155
Come, bring me where they are.

                                        Exeunt.

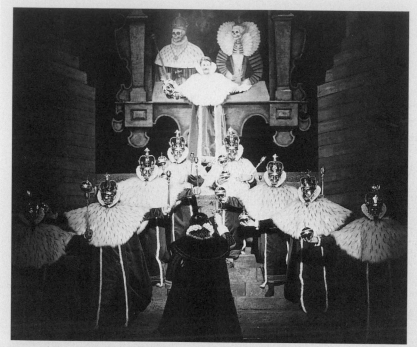

National Theatre, 1972

RSC, 1993

National Theatre, 1972

Ludlow Festival, 2001

In this scene ...

- Ross visits Lady Macduff. She cannot understand why her husband has left her to flee to England.
- After Ross leaves, a frightened messenger urges Lady Macduff to escape from the approaching danger.
- Murderers kill Lady Macduff's son and chase her as she tries to escape.

In Macduff's castle, Lady Macduff tells Ross that her husband showed little thought for his family when he fled to England. Ross tries to explain the reason for Macduff's actions.

3–4 **When ... traitors**: i.e. Even though Macduff was not a traitor, running away made him look like one

7 **titles**: lands and possessions owned as Thane of Fife

9 **wants ... touch**: i.e. lacks the normal feelings of a father and husband

12 **All ... love**: His actions are motivated totally by fear, not by love for his family

14 **runs ... reason**: goes against common sense
coz: cousin (or any close relative)

15 **school yourself**: learn to live with it / control yourself

16 **judicious**: possesses sound judgement

17 **The ... season**: the way things violently change these days

19 **And ... ourselves**: without realising it
hold rumour: believe rumours

22 **Each ... move**: and are swept this way and that

24 **climb upward**: get better

Think about

- In the Roman Polanski film, Ross was portrayed as deceitful and treacherous, but in most productions he is loyal and honest. If you were the director, how would you want him to be played?

Fife: inside Macduff's castle.

Enter LADY MACDUFF, *and her young* SON, *with* ROSS.

LADY MACDUFF What had he done, to make him fly the land?

ROSS You must have patience, madam.

LADY MACDUFF   *He* had none:
His flight was madness. When our actions do not,
Our fears do make us traitors.

ROSS   You know not
Whether it was his wisdom or his fear.   5

LADY MACDUFF Wisdom! – to leave his wife, to leave his babes,
His mansion and his titles, in a place
From whence himself does fly? He loves us not.
He wants the natural touch – for the poor wren,
The most diminutive of birds, will fight,   10
Her young ones in her nest, against the owl.
All is the fear, and nothing is the love;
As little is the wisdom, where the flight
So runs against all reason.

ROSS   My dearest coz,
I pray you, school yourself. But for your husband,   15
He is noble, wise, judicious, and best knows
The fits o' the season. I dare not speak much further:
But cruel are the times, when we are traitors,
And do not know ourselves – when we hold rumour
From what we fear, yet know not what we fear,   20
But float upon a wild and violent sea
Each way, and move. – I take my leave of you:
Shall not be long but I'll be here again.
Things at the worst will cease, or else climb upward
To what they were before. – *(To the* SON*)* My pretty
    cousin,   25
Blessing upon you!

LADY MACDUFF Fathered he is, and yet he's fatherless.

When Ross leaves, Lady
Macduff tells her son that his
father is dead, but the boy
refuses to believe her.

29 It … discomfort: i.e. I fear I will start
to weep

30 Sirrah: i.e. Boy

34 lime: sticky substance for trapping
birds
35 pit-fall: covered hole / trap
gin: snare
36 Poor … for: i.e. They are only set for
rich and powerful people

42 wit: intelligence
43 And … thee: it isn't much, but it's not
bad for a child of your age

Think about

• What does the conversation
between Lady Macduff and
her son add here? For
example, how might it
change our view of
Macduff? Why is it
important for us to see Lady
Macduff and her son before
the murderers arrive?

47 swears and lies: takes an oath and
breaks it
48 be … so: are all people who do that
traitors

ROSS	I am so much a fool, should I stay longer,
	It would be my disgrace and your discomfort.
	I take my leave at once.

Exit.

LADY MACDUFF   Sirrah, your father's dead: **30**
And what will you do now? How will you live?

SON   As birds do, mother.

LADY MACDUFF   What, with worms and flies?

SON   With what I get, I mean – and so do they.

LADY MACDUFF Poor bird! Thou'dst never fear the net, nor lime,
The pit-fall, nor the gin?

SON   Why should I, mother?   **35**
Poor birds they are not set for.
My father is *not* dead, for all your saying.

LADY MACDUFF Yes, he is dead. How wilt thou do for a father?

SON   Nay, how will *you* do for a husband?

LADY MACDUFF Why, I can buy me twenty at any market.   **40**

SON   Then you'll buy 'em to sell again.

LADY MACDUFF Thou speakest with all thy wit –
And yet, i' faith, with wit enough for thee.

SON   Was my father a traitor, mother?

LADY MACDUFF Ay, that he was.   **45**

SON   What is a traitor?

LADY MACDUFF Why, one that swears and lies.

SON   And be all traitors that do so?

LADY MACDUFF Every one that does so is a traitor, and must be hanged.

SON   And must they all be hanged that swear and lie?   **50**

LADY MACDUFF Every one.

SON   Who must hang them?

LADY MACDUFF Why, the honest men.

A messenger arrives and warns Lady Macduff that danger is approaching. While Lady Macduff is thinking about what to do, murderers burst in, asking for Macduff.

59 **would not**: i.e. didn't weep for him

62 **prattler**: chatterbox

64 **in your ... perfect**: I know your rank perfectly well
65 **doubt**: suspect
66 **homely**: humble
67 **Hence**: Get away from here
68 **savage**: cruel
69 **fell**: terrible
70 **nigh**: close to
71 **abide**: stay
    Whither ... fly: Where could I run away to

---Think about---

• Like the old man in Act 2 Scene 4, the third murderer in Act 3 Scene 3, and the lord in Act 3 Scene 6, we don't know who the messenger is. What are the advantages of (a) keeping him anonymous; and (b) showing him to be a character we have seen earlier in the play?

74 **laudable**: praiseworthy
75 **Accounted**: considered
    folly: foolishness / stupidity

79 **unsanctified**: unholy

81 **shag-haired**: i.e. scruffy

| SON | Then the liars and swearers are fools. For there are liars and swearers enough to beat the honest men, and hang up them. | 55 |

| LADY MACDUFF | Now God help thee, poor monkey! But how wilt thou do for a father? |

| SON | If he were dead, you'd weep for him. If you would not, it were a good sign that I should quickly have a new father. | 60 |

| LADY MACDUFF | Poor prattler, how thou talk'st! |

Enter a MESSENGER.

MESSENGER	Bless you, fair dame! I am not to you known,
	Though in your state of honour I am perfect.
	I doubt some danger does approach you nearly.	65
	If you will take a homely man's advice,
	Be not found here. Hence, with your little ones.
	To fright you thus, methinks, I am too savage;
	To do worse to you were fell cruelty,
	Which is too nigh your person. Heaven preserve you!	70
	I dare abide no longer.

Exit.

LADY MACDUFF	Whither should I fly?
	I have done no harm. But I remember now
	I am in this earthly world, where to do harm
	Is often laudable, to do good sometime
	Accounted dangerous folly. Why then, alas,	75
	Do I put up that womanly defence,
	To say I have done no harm? –

Enter MURDERERS.

| | What are these faces? |

| MURDERER | Where is your husband? |

| LADY MACDUFF | I hope in no place so unsanctified, |
| | Where such as thou may'st find him. |

| MURDERER | He's a traitor. | 80 |

| SON | Thou liest, thou shag-haired villain! |

The men kill Lady Macduff's son and chase after her as she tries to escape.

81–2   egg … fry: insulting terms for offspring or small children

┌─**Think about**────────

• Before this scene begins, we already know that Macbeth is a bloody murderer. So what effect does the scene have? How might it affect an audience's feelings?

MURDERER   What, you egg! –

Stabbing him.

Young fry of treachery!

SON   He has killed me, mother.
Run away, I pray you!

Dies.

Exit LADY MACDUFF, *crying out 'Murder!', with the* MURDERERS
pursuing her.

ACT 4   SCENE 3

In this scene ...

- In England, Macduff hopes to persuade Malcolm to return to Scotland and overthrow Macbeth.
- Having tested Macduff's loyalty, Malcolm reveals that he has an army and is prepared to invade.
- Ross arrives and tells Macduff that his family has been killed.
- Malcolm tries to comfort Macduff and they prepare to march north to do battle with Macbeth.

In England, Malcolm is visited by Macduff who wants him to lead an army back to Scotland and overthrow Macbeth. Malcolm is suspicious, fearing that Macduff might have been sent by Macbeth and might betray him to Macbeth for personal reward.

Think about

- What is the effect of the dramatic irony in what Macduff says in lines 4 to 8, and Malcolm's 'He hath not touched you yet' (line 14)?

2 **bosoms**: hearts

3 **mortal**: deadly

4 **Bestride ... birthdom**: defend the fallen kingdom of our birth

6 **that it resounds**: so that it echoes

8 **Like ... dolour**: a similar mournful noise
wail: weep for

9 **redress**: put right

10 **the ... friend**: the times are favourable

11 **perchance**: perhaps

12 **sole**: mere

14–15 **but ... me**: but you might be able to use me to get some reward from him

15 **wisdom**: i.e. you might think it wise

16 **weak ... lamb**: i.e. Macduff might offer Malcolm to Macbeth as a sacrifice

17 **appease**: calm the anger of

19–20 **may recoil ... charge**: may behave wickedly on the orders of a king

21 **transpose**: change

22 **the brightest fell**: the brightest angel, Lucifer, became a devil

23–4 **Though ... so**: Although evil people try to appear good, many others who appear virtuous genuinely are so

26 **rawness**: unprotected state

27 **motives**: people inspiring love, i.e. Macduff's wife and children

England: the palace of King Edward.

Enter MALCOLM, *with* MACDUFF.

MALCOLM   Let us seek out some desolate shade, and there
      Weep our sad bosoms empty.

MACDUFF   Let us rather
      Hold fast the mortal sword, and like good men
      Bestride our down-fall birthdom. Each new morn,
      New widows howl, new orphans cry. New sorrows   5
      Strike heaven on the face, that it resounds
      As if it felt with Scotland, and yelled out
      Like syllable of dolour.

MALCOLM   What I believe, I'll wail;
      What know, believe; and what I can redress –
      As I shall find the time to friend, I will.   10
      What you have spoke, it may be so, perchance.
      This tyrant, whose sole name blisters our tongues,
      Was once thought honest: you have loved him well.
      He hath not touched you yet. I am young – but
        something
      You may deserve of him through me, and wisdom 15
      To offer up a weak, poor, innocent lamb,
      To appease an angry god.

MACDUFF   I am not treacherous.

MALCOLM   But Macbeth is.
      A good and virtuous nature may recoil
      In an imperial charge. But I shall crave your pardon: 20
      That which you are, my thoughts cannot transpose.
      Angels are bright still, though the brightest fell.
      Though all things foul would wear the brows of grace,
      Yet grace must still look so.

MACDUFF   I have lost my hopes.

MALCOLM   Perchance even there, where I did find my doubts. 25
      Why in that rawness left you wife and child
      (Those precious motives, those strong knots of love)

Macduff is upset that Malcolm should suspect him of trying to deceive him. Still unsure whether or not Macduff can be trusted, Malcolm tests his loyalty by pretending that he himself is full of faults and vices.

29–30 Let ... safeties: I am not suspicious because you have behaved dishonourably, but because I fear for my own safety

30 rightly just: genuinely honest

32 lay ... sure: you can lay secure foundations

33 goodness ... thee: good people are afraid to stop you
Wear ... wrongs: Display your evil deeds openly

34 affeered: legally confirmed

36 space: country

37 to boot: as well

39 sinks ... yoke: is dragged down by tyranny

41 withal: in addition to this

42 hands ... right: people willing to fight on my side
gracious England: i.e. King Edward the Confessor

46 wear ... sword: i.e. cut off Macbeth's head and spear it on the end of my sword

48 sundry: varied

49 What ... be: Who are you talking about

51 All ... grafted: all the individual vices are so firmly rooted in me

52 shall be opened: are revealed

54 Esteem: judge

55 confineless harms: boundless evils
legions: armies of devils

57 top: outdo in evils

Think about

• What is Malcolm suspicious of? Look, for example, at his comment to Macduff 'He hath not touched you yet' (line 14), as well as lines 14 to 17, and 19 to 28.

Without leave-taking? – I pray you,
Let not my jealousies be your dishonours,
But mine own safeties. You may be rightly just,   30
Whatever I shall think.

MACDUFF   Bleed, bleed, poor country!
Great tyranny, lay thou thy basis sure,
For goodness dare not check thee! Wear thou thy
     wrongs –
The title is affeered! – Fare thee well, lord.
I would not be the villain that thou think'st   35
For the whole space that's in the tyrant's grasp,
And the rich East to boot.

MALCOLM   Be not offended.
I speak not as in absolute fear of you.
I think our country sinks beneath the yoke:
It weeps, it bleeds – and each new day a gash   40
Is added to her wounds. I think, withal,
There would be hands uplifted in my right;
And here, from gracious England, have I offer
Of goodly thousands. But, for all this,
When I shall tread upon the tyrant's head,   45
Or wear it on my sword, yet my poor country
Shall have more vices than it had before,
More suffer, and more sundry ways than ever,
By him that shall succeed.

MACDUFF   What should he be?

MALCOLM   It is myself I mean – in whom I know   50
All the particulars of vice so grafted,
That, when they shall be opened, black Macbeth
Will seem as pure as snow – and the poor state
Esteem him as a lamb, being compared
With *my* confineless harms.

MACDUFF   Not in the legions   55
Of horrid hell can come a devil more damned
In evils, to top Macbeth.

Malcolm pretends that, as King, he would be even more wicked than Macbeth. He claims to be lustful and greedy. Macduff replies that Malcolm's weaknesses could be tolerated, given his good qualities.

58 **Luxurious**: lustful
avaricious: greedy
59 **Sudden**: unpredictably violent
smacking of: having a 'taste' of
61 **voluptuousness**: sexual appetite
62 **matrons**: older women
62–3 **fill … cistern of**: i.e. satisfy
64 **All … o'erbear**: would burst through any barriers
65 **will**: sexual desire
66 **intemperance**: lack of control
67–8 **been … throne**: caused many a happy reign to come to an early end

71 **Convey … plenty**: enjoy secretly
72 **seem cold**: appear to be sexually pure
the time … hoodwink: you could deceive people in that way
75–6 **As … inclined**: who would offer themselves to their king, if he had such desires

77 **ill-composed affection**: character made up of bad qualities
78 **staunchless avarice**: endless greed
79 **cut off**: kill
81–2 **my … more**: the more I had, the more I would want

84–5 **This … deeper**: This greed is a more serious weakness
85 **pernicious**: destructive
86 **summer-seeming**: i.e. which fades as you grow older
87 **sword**: i.e. reason for killing
88 **foisons**: wealth
89 **Of … own**: even if you count just your own royal possessions
these: i.e. these vices
portable: bearable

Think about

• Look at the list of sins which Macbeth is guilty of, according to Malcolm (lines 57 to 59). What evidence is there for each one in the play?

MALCOLM   I grant him bloody,
           Luxurious, avaricious, false, deceitful,
           Sudden, malicious, smacking of every sin
           That has a name. But there's no bottom, none,   60
           In *my* voluptuousness: your wives, your daughters,
           Your matrons and your maids, could not fill up
           The cistern of my lust – and my desire
           All continent impediments would o'erbear,
           That did oppose my will. Better Macbeth   65
           Than such an one to reign.

MACDUFF   Boundless intemperance
           In nature is a tyranny: it hath been
           Th' untimely emptying of the happy throne,
           And fall of many kings. But fear not yet
           To take upon you what is yours. You may   70
           Convey your pleasures in a spacious plenty,
           And yet seem cold – the time you may so hoodwink.
           We have willing dames enough – there cannot be
           That vulture in you, to devour so many
           As will to greatness dedicate themselves,   75
           Finding it so inclined.

MALCOLM   With this, there grows
           In my most ill-composed affection such
           A staunchless avarice, that, were I King,
           I should cut off the nobles for their lands –
           Desire his jewels, and this other's house.   80
           And my more-having would be as a sauce
           To make me hunger more, that I should forge
           Quarrels unjust against the good and loyal,
           Destroying them for wealth.

MACDUFF   This avarice
           Sticks deeper, grows with more pernicious root   85
           Than summer-seeming lust – and it hath been
           The sword of our slain kings. Yet do not fear.
           Scotland hath foisons to fill up your will,
           Of your mere own. All these are portable,
           With other graces weighed.   90

Malcolm continues his test of Macduff's loyalty. He claims to lack all the good characteristics a king should possess. Macduff finally believes Malcolm and angrily rejects him as a fit ruler. This is the reassurance that Malcolm wanted.

91 king-becoming graces: virtues which a king ought to have
92 verity: truthfulness
temperance: moderation
93 Bounty: generosity
94 Devotion: love of God
fortitude: strength of character
95 relish: trace
95–6 abound … crime: have lots of variations on each individual sin
98 concord: peace and harmony
99 Uproar: throw into confusion
confound: destroy

104 untitled: with no legal right to the throne

106 issue of: heir to
107 interdiction: accusation
108 does … breed: slanders his family
111 Died … lived: constantly prepared herself for heaven
112–13 thou … Scotland: 1 you report about yourself; 2 which are the same as Macbeth's
115 Child of integrity: i.e. which comes from your honest character
116 black scruples: sinister suspicions
118 trains: tricks / plots
119–20 modest … haste: cautious good sense holds me back from believing people too hastily
121 Deal … me: i.e. bless our relationship
123 Unspeak … detraction: take back everything I said against myself
abjure: deny
124 taints … myself: the sins and crimes I accused myself of
125 For … nature: i.e. as things that are not part of my character

Think about

• Which aspects of the behaviour described by Malcolm, in lines 60 to 65, 76 to 84, and 91 to 100, would be most likely to persuade Macduff – and Shakespeare's audience – that such a man was not fit to rule?

MALCOLM	But I have none. The king-becoming graces –
	As justice, verity, temperance, stableness,
	Bounty, perseverance, mercy, lowliness,
	Devotion, patience, courage, fortitude –

MALCOLM But I have none. The king-becoming graces –
As justice, verity, temperance, stableness,
Bounty, perseverance, mercy, lowliness,
Devotion, patience, courage, fortitude –
I have no relish of them; but abound   95
In the division of each several crime,
Acting it many ways. Nay, had I power, I should
Pour the sweet milk of concord into hell,
Uproar the universal peace, confound
All unity on earth.

MACDUFF   O Scotland! Scotland!   100

MALCOLM If such a one be fit to govern, speak.
I am as I have spoken.

MACDUFF   Fit to govern?
No, not to live! – O nation miserable! –
With an untitled tyrant, bloody-sceptered!
When shalt thou see thy wholesome days again,   105
Since that the truest issue of thy throne
By his own interdiction stands accused,
And does blaspheme his breed? Thy royal father
Was a most sainted King. The Queen that bore thee,
Oft'ner upon her knees than on her feet,   110
Died every day she lived. Fare thee well!
These evils thou repeat'st upon thyself
Hath banished me from Scotland. – O my breast,
Thy hope ends here!

MALCOLM   Macduff, this noble passion,
Child of integrity, hath from my soul   115
Wiped the black scruples, reconciled my thoughts
To thy good truth and honour. Devilish Macbeth
By many of these trains hath sought to win me
Into his power, and modest wisdom plucks me
From over-credulous haste. But God above   120
Deal between thee and me! For even now
I put myself to thy direction, and
Unspeak mine own detraction – here abjure
The taints and blames I laid upon myself
For strangers to my nature. I am yet   125

Malcolm explains that he was lying to test Macduff's loyalty. A doctor enters and they discuss the power of Edward the Confessor, the English King, to cure a disease known as 'the king's evil'.

126   **Unknown to woman**: a virgin
      never was forsworn: have never lied
127   **coveted**: been envious of
128   **my faith**: a promise I had made

133   **Whither**: to Scotland
      here-approach: arrival
135   **at a point**: fully prepared for battle
136–7 **chance … quarrel**: may our chance of success be equal to the justice of our cause

139   **reconcile**: adjust my mind to
      more anon: we'll talk more later

142   **stay his cure**: are waiting to be cured by him
      malady: disease
142–3 **convinces … art**: defeats the greatest medical skill
144   **sanctity**: holy power
145   **presently amend**: instantly recover
146   **the Evil**: scrofula, a disease that English kings were said to be able to cure by touching
148   **here-remain**: stay
149   **solicits**: gets help from
150   **strangely-visited**: with strange illnesses
152   **mere … surgery**: people that doctors have completely given up on
153   **stamp**: coin
154   **'tis spoken**: it is said
155–6 **leaves … benediction**: hands on this blessed power
156   **With … virtue**: As well as this strange talent

Think about

• Edward the Confessor is called 'this good king': he 'solicits heaven', he cures the sick, he has the gift of prophecy, and he is famous for his virtues (lines 141 to 159). In what ways might each of these qualities or actions be contrasted with Macbeth's?

Unknown to woman; never was forsworn;
Scarcely have coveted what was mine own;
At no time broke my faith: would not betray
The devil to his fellow – and delight
No less in truth than life. My first false speaking   **130**
Was this upon myself. What I am truly
Is thine, and my poor country's, to command –
Whither, indeed, before thy here-approach,
Old Siward, with ten thousand warlike men,
Already at a point, was setting forth.   **135**
Now we'll together, and the chance of goodness
Be like our warranted quarrel! Why are you silent?

MACDUFF   Such welcome and unwelcome things at once,
'Tis hard to reconcile.

Enter an English DOCTOR.

MALCOLM   Well, more anon. –
(*To the* DOCTOR) Comes the King forth, I pray you?   **140**

DOCTOR   Ay, sir. There are a crew of wretched souls
That stay his cure. Their malady convinces
The great assay of art – but, at his touch,
Such sanctity hath heaven given his hand,
They presently amend.

MALCOLM   I thank you, doctor.   **145**

Exit DOCTOR.

MACDUFF   What's the disease he means?

MALCOLM   'Tis called the Evil.
A most miraculous work in this good King,
Which often, since my here-remain in England,
I have seen him do. How he solicits heaven
Himself best knows; but strangely-visited people,   **150**
All swoll'n and ulcerous, pitiful to the eye,
The mere despair of surgery, he cures –
Hanging a golden stamp about their necks,
Put on with holy prayers. And 'tis spoken,
To the succeeding royalty he leaves   **155**
The healing benediction. With this strange virtue

167

Ross arrives with the latest news from Scotland. He describes the country's suffering under Macbeth, but then lies, telling Macduff that his family are well.

158 **sundry**: various
159 **speak him**: declare that he is

162 **betimes**: quickly
163 **means**: conditions

164 **Stands ... did**: Are things still the same in Scotland

166–7 **nothing ... smile**: the only cheerful people are those who know nothing
168 **rend**: tear apart / split
169 **not marked**: but nobody takes any notice of them
170 **modern ecstasy**: common emotion
170–1 **The ... who:** When the funeral bell tolls, people hardly bother to ask who it is for
172 **Expire**: come to an end
173 **or ... sicken**: before they have time to fall ill and die naturally
173–4 **relation ... nice**: this report has too many ugly details
175 **That ... speaker**: Anyone telling hour-old news will be booed by their audience
176 **teems ... one**: gives rise to fresh suffering

179 **well at peace**: can mean 'dead'

Think about

• Why do you think that Ross initially reports that Macduff's wife and children are well (lines 176 to 179)? Which words and phrases in his replies can have more than one meaning?

• What picture of Scotland under Macbeth is presented by Macduff and Malcolm in this scene?

He hath a heavenly gift of prophecy;
And sundry blessings hang about his throne
That speak him full of grace.

Enter ROSS.

MACDUFF	See, who comes here?	
MALCOLM	My countryman – but yet I know him not.	**160**
MACDUFF	My ever-gentle cousin, welcome hither!	
MALCOLM	I know him now. Good God betimes remove	
	The means that makes us strangers!	
ROSS	Sir, amen.	
MACDUFF	Stands Scotland where it did?	
ROSS	Alas, poor country! –	
	Almost afraid to know itself. It cannot	**165**
	Be called our mother, but our grave – where nothing,	
	But who knows nothing, is once seen to smile;	
	Where sighs, and groans, and shrieks that rend the air	
	Are made, not marked; where violent sorrow seems	
	A modern ecstasy. The dead man's knell	**170**
	Is there scarce asked for who – and good men's lives	
	Expire before the flowers in their caps,	
	Dying or ere they sicken.	
MACDUFF	O relation	
	Too nice and yet too true!	
MALCOLM	What's the newest grief?	
ROSS	That of an hour's age doth hiss the speaker:	**175**
	Each minute teems a new one.	
MACDUFF	How does my wife?	
ROSS	Why, well.	
MACDUFF	And all my children?	
ROSS	Well, too.	
MACDUFF	The tyrant has not battered at their peace?	
ROSS	No. They were well at peace when I did leave 'em.	

Ross reports that many good men are preparing to rebel against Macbeth. Malcolm confirms his plan to invade Scotland with the support of an English army. Ross now reveals to Macduff that his family have been murdered.

Think about

- If you were the director, how would you ask the actor playing Ross to act in lines 180 to 213? Think about how he should deliver the reports about Scotland to encourage Malcolm, and then break the news to Macduff of his family's killing.

180 **Be not … speech:** Don't hold back

183 **out**: i.e. preparing for battle
184–5 **was … that**: I was more prepared to believe because
185 **power afoot**: army on the march
186 **eye**: appearance

188 **doff … distresses**: throw off their terrible miseries

191–2 **none … out**: the Christian world cannot boast of
192 **Would**: I wish

195 **latch**: catch

196 **The general cause**: Is this bad news for everybody
196–7 **fee-grief … breast**: personal sorrow

199 **Pertains**: belongs

202 **possess**: inform

204 **is surprised**: has been taken by surprise

206 **Were**: would be
on the … deer: i.e. onto the pile of Macduff's slaughtered family

MACDUFF	Be not a niggard of your speech: how goes 't? **180**
ROSS	When I came hither to transport the tidings
	Which I have heavily borne, there ran a rumour
	Of many worthy fellows that were out –
	Which was, to my belief, witnessed the rather
	For that I saw the tyrant's power afoot. **185**
	Now is the time of help. (*To* MALCOLM) Your eye in
	Scotland
	Would create soldiers, make our women fight
	To doff their dire distresses.

MALCOLM   Be 't their comfort,
We are coming thither. Gracious England hath
Lent us good Siward, and ten thousand men –   **190**
An older and a better soldier none
That Christendom gives out.

ROSS   Would I could answer
This comfort with the like! But I have words
That would be howled out in the desert air,
Where hearing should not latch them.

MACDUFF   What concern they? **195**
The general cause? Or is it a fee-grief
Due to some single breast?

ROSS   No mind that's honest
But in it shares some woe, though the main part
Pertains to you alone.

MACDUFF   If it be mine,
Keep it not from me: quickly let me have it.   **200**

ROSS   Let not your ears despise my tongue for ever,
Which shall possess them with the heaviest sound
That ever yet they heard.

MACDUFF   H'm! – I guess at it.

ROSS   Your castle is surprised – your wife and babes
Savagely slaughtered. To relate the manner   **205**
Were, on the quarry of these murdered deer,
To add the death of you.

Malcolm tries to comfort
Macduff over the loss of his
family.

208 Ne'er ... hat: a sign of grief

210 o'er-fraught: overloaded

212 must ... thence: had to be away from
home

217 hell-kite: like a bird of prey from hell
218 dam: mother
219 fell: deadly

Dispute: Fight

223 take their part: fight on their side
224 Naught that: Worthless as
225 demerits: faults

227 whetstone: tool used for sharpening
knives and swords
228 Blunt ... heart: i.e. Don't let grief
deaden your spirits
229 play the: behave like a
230 braggart: boaster
231 Cut ... intermission: let there be no
interval
Front to front: Face to face

Think about

- Who is Macduff referring to
when he says 'He has no
children' (line 216) –
Malcolm or Macbeth?

- In what ways is the debate
about manhood, and what
it means to be 'a man',
developed here? Look at
Malcolm's statements and
Macduff's replies.

MALCOLM	Merciful heaven! –
	What, man! Ne'er pull your hat upon your brows:
	Give sorrow words. The grief that does not speak
	Whispers the o'er-fraught heart, and bids it break.

210

MACDUFF	My children too?

ROSS	Wife, children, servants – all
	That could be found.

MACDUFF	And I must be from thence!
	My wife killed too?

ROSS	I have said.

MALCOLM	Be comforted.
	Let's make us medicines of our great revenge,
	To cure this deadly grief.

215

MACDUFF	He has no children. – All my pretty ones?
	Did you say all? – O hell-kite! – All?
	What, all my pretty chickens, and their dam,
	At one fell swoop?

MALCOLM	Dispute it like a man.

MACDUFF	I shall do so.
	But I must also feel it as a man:
	I cannot but remember such things were,
	That were most precious to me. – Did heaven look on,
	And would not take their part? Sinful Macduff!
	They were all struck for thee. Naught that I am,
	Not for their own demerits, but for mine
	Fell slaughter on their souls. Heaven rest them now!

220

225

MALCOLM	Be this the whetstone of your sword: let grief
	Convert to anger. Blunt not the heart, enrage it.

MACDUFF	O! I could play the woman with mine eyes,
	And braggart with my tongue. – But, gentle heavens,
	Cut short all intermission. Front to front
	Bring thou this fiend of Scotland and myself.
	Within my sword's length set him. If he 'scape,
	Heaven forgive him too!

230

Malcolm goes off with Macduff and Ross to prepare for the attack on Macbeth.

234 **This ... manly**: i.e. That's a man's reaction
235 **power**: army
236 **Our ... leave**: All that remains for us to do is leave
237 **ripe for shaking**: i.e. like ripe fruit ready to be shaken from the tree
above: in heaven
238 **Put ... instruments**: are arming themselves
cheer: comfort
239 **The ... day**: it's a long night that has no dawn

Think about

• What impression have you received of Malcolm from this scene? Look, for example, at the way he deals with Macduff, and at his final speech (lines 234 to 239). What kind of king is he likely to be?

• If you were the director, would you stage this scene in light, pleasant surroundings or in gloom? What effect could each setting have?

MALCOLM   This tune goes manly.
Come, go we to the King. Our power is ready –   **235**
Our lack is nothing but our leave. Macbeth
Is ripe for shaking, and the powers above
Put on their instruments. Receive what cheer you may:
The night is long that never finds the day.

Exeunt.

In this scene ...

- Lady Macbeth's doctor and gentlewoman watch her sleepwalking.
- They see that her mind is tormented by guilt and horror at the murders that have been committed.

Lady Macbeth's gentlewoman tells a doctor about her strange behaviour. She appears, walking in her sleep.

Think about

- If you were the director, what advice would you give to the actress playing Lady Macbeth about this scene? Think about her movements and actions, how she should speak the lines, where she should pause, her facial expressions, and what emotions the character is experiencing.

- What do you think Lady Macbeth writes on the paper mentioned by her gentlewoman (lines 3 to 7)?

1   **watched**: kept watch

3   **went ... field**: led his army (against the rebels)
5   **closet**: private chest for valuables

8   **perturbation in nature**: disorder in her mind and body
     at once: at the same time
9   **do ... watching**: behave as though awake
10 **slumbery agitation**: physical activity while asleep
11 **actual performances**: things you have actually seen her do
13 **after her**: that she said
14 **most meet**: appropriate

17 **Lo you**: Look
     her very guise: the way she behaved before
18 **stand close**: keep out of sight

23 **their ... shut**: i.e. she is not actually seeing anything

25 **accustomed**: usual / frequent

Inside Macbeth's castle at Dunsinane.

Enter a DOCTOR, *with a* WAITING-GENTLEWOMAN.

DOCTOR   I have two nights watched with you, but can perceive
                no truth in your report. When was it she last walked?

GENTLEWOMAN   Since his Majesty went into the field, I have seen
                her rise from her bed, throw her night-gown upon her,
                unlock her closet, take forth paper, fold it, write upon 't,   5
                read it, afterwards seal it, and again return to bed – yet
                all this while in a most fast sleep.

DOCTOR   A great perturbation in nature, to receive at once the
                benefit of sleep, and do the effects of watching! In this
                slumbery agitation, besides her walking and other   10
                actual performances, what, at any time, have you heard
                her say?

GENTLEWOMAN   That, sir, which I will not report after her.

DOCTOR   You may to me; and 'tis most meet you should.

GENTLEWOMAN   Neither to you, nor any one, having no witness to   15
                confirm my speech.

        Enter LADY MACBETH *in her night-gown, with a candle.*

                Lo you! Here she comes. This is her very guise – and,
                upon my life, fast asleep. Observe her: stand close.

DOCTOR   How came she by that light?

GENTLEWOMAN   Why, it stood by her. She has light by her continually –   20
                'tis her command.

DOCTOR   You see, her eyes are open.

GENTLEWOMAN   Ay, but their sense are shut.

DOCTOR   What is it she does now? Look, how she rubs her hands.

GENTLEWOMAN   It is an accustomed action with her, to seem thus   25
                washing her hands. I have known her continue
                in this a quarter of an hour.

In her sleepwalking Lady Macbeth imagines that she is washing blood off her hands. It seems that she is talking to her husband in her sleep about the murders that he and his followers have committed.

29 **set**: write
30 **satisfy my remembrance**: back up my memory
31 **One, two**: She imagines she hears a bell (see Act 2 Scene 1, line 63).
32 **Fie**: Shame on you
33 **afeard**: afraid
34 **none … account**: we are so powerful that nobody can challenge what we have done
37 **mark**: hear
38 **Thane of Fife:** i.e. Macduff

40 **mar all**: ruin everything
41 **starting**: nervousness / jumpiness

42 **Go to**: i.e. That's bad

47 **sorely charged**: carrying a heavy burden (of guilt)
49 **dignity**: worth / value

52 **practice**: skill as a doctor
53–4 **died holily**: i.e. with clear consciences

57 **on's**: of his
58 **Even so**: So is that the way things are

Think about

- In a film version, it would be possible to show what is going on in Lady Macbeth's head. How could this be done and what images might be shown?

LADY MACBETH Yet here's a spot.

DOCTOR Hark! She speaks. I will set down what comes from her, to satisfy my remembrance the more strongly.   30

LADY MACBETH Out, damned spot! Out, I say! – One, two. Why, then 'tis time to do it. – Hell is murky. – Fie, my lord, fie! – a soldier, and afeard? – What need we fear who knows it, when none can call our power to account? – Yet who would have thought the old man to have had so much   35 blood in him?

DOCTOR Do you mark that?

LADY MACBETH The Thane of Fife had a wife: where is she now? – What, will these hands ne'er be clean? – No more o' that, my lord, no more o' that: you mar all with this   40 starting.

DOCTOR Go to, go to: you have known what you should not.

GENTLEWOMAN She has spoke what she should not, I am sure of that. Heaven knows what she has known.

LADY MACBETH Here's the smell of the blood still! All the perfumes of   45 Arabia will not sweeten this little hand. O! Oh, oh –

DOCTOR What a sigh is there! The heart is sorely charged.

GENTLEWOMAN I would not have such a heart in my bosom for the dignity of the whole body.

DOCTOR Well, well, well –   50

GENTLEWOMAN Pray God it be, sir.

DOCTOR This disease is beyond my practice. Yet I have known those which have walked in their sleep, who have died holily in their beds.

LADY MACBETH Wash your hands, put on your night-gown. Look   55 not so pale. – I tell you yet again, Banquo's buried: he cannot come out on's grave.

DOCTOR Even so?

Lady Macbeth goes back to bed and the Doctor leaves, shocked by what he has seen and heard.

63 **Directly**: Immediately

64 **Foul ... abroad**: Terrible rumours are going around

65 **infected**: diseased

66 **discharge**: reveal

67 **More ... physician**: She needs a priest more than a doctor

69 **means ... annoyance**: anything that she might harm herself with

70 **still**: always

71 **mated**: bewildered

Think about

- Minor characters in Shakespeare's plays are often extremely important. What does the Doctor say in his final speech (lines 64 to 72) which adds to our understanding of Scotland under Macbeth's rule?

- What events earlier in the play do Lady Macbeth's speeches and actions in this scene refer to?

LADY MACBETH To bed, to bed: there's knocking at the gate! Come, come, come, come, give me your hand. What's done **60** cannot be undone. To bed, to bed, to bed.

Exit.

DOCTOR Will she go now to bed?

GENTLEWOMAN Directly.

DOCTOR Foul whisp'rings are abroad. Unnatural deeds
Do breed unnatural troubles: infected minds **65**
To their deaf pillows will discharge their secrets.
More needs she the divine than the physician. –
God, God forgive us all! Look after her.
Remove from her the means of all annoyance,
And still keep eyes upon her. – So, goodnight. **70**
My mind she has mated, and amazed my sight.
I think, but dare not speak.

GENTLEWOMAN   Goodnight, good doctor.

Exeunt.

RSC, 2004

National Theatre, 1972

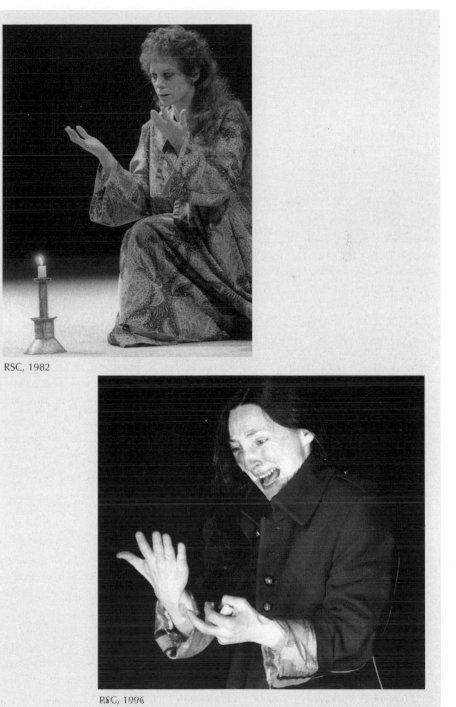

RSC, 1982

RSC, 1996

In this scene ...

- The army of Scottish lords formed to overthrow Macbeth approaches Macbeth's castle at Dunsinane, ready to meet up with Malcolm.
- The lords discuss Macbeth's loss of control.

The army of Scottish lords marches to join up with Malcolm, Macduff and the English forces. They discuss reports that Macbeth has taken refuge in his castle, and that people are now following him out of fear, not loyalty.

Think about

- What does the clothing imagery in lines 15 to 22 tell us about the Thanes' opinions of (a) Macbeth's control of his kingdom; and (b) his fitness to bear the great title of King?

1 **power**: army

3 **their dear causes**: the terrible wrongs done against them
4–5 **to the ... man**: be enough to make a dead or paralysed man want to join in the bloodshed and din of battle
6 **well**: probably

8 **file**: list
9 **gentry**: noblemen
10 **unrough**: unbearded, i.e. young
11 **Protest ... manhood**: show that they are now acting like men for the first time

14 **valiant fury**: mad courage
15 **distempered**: swollen with disease

18 **Now ... faith-breach**: Every minute rebellions attack him for his disloyalty
19–20 **move ... love**: only obey him because they are following orders, not because they love him
23 **pestered senses**: troubled nerves
   to recoil and start: i.e. for being jumpy
24–5 **all ... there**: i.e. his whole inner being is sickened at the thought of what he has become

Open country near Dunsinane.

Enter soldiers, with drums beating and banners.

Enter MENTEITH, CAITHNESS, ANGUS, *and* LENNOX.

MENTEITH	The English power is near, led on by Malcolm,
	His uncle Siward, and the good Macduff.
	Revenges burn in them – for their dear causes
	Would to the bleeding and the grim alarm
	Excite the mortified man.

ANGUS   Near Birnam wood   5
Shall we well meet them: that way are they coming.

CAITHNESS   Who knows if Donalbain be with his brother?

LENNOX   For certain, sir, he is not. I have a file
Of all the gentry. There is Siward's son,
And many unrough youths, that even now   10
Protest their first of manhood.

MENTEITH   What does the tyrant?

CAITHNESS   Great Dunsinane he strongly fortifies.
Some say he's mad. Others, that lesser hate him,
Do call it valiant fury – but for certain,
He cannot buckle his distempered cause   15
Within the belt of rule.

ANGUS   Now does he feel
His secret murders sticking on his hands.
Now minutely revolts upbraid his faith-breach:
Those he commands move only in command,
Nothing in love. Now does he feel his title   20
Hang loose about him, like a giant's robe
Upon a dwarfish thief.

MENTEITH   Who then shall blame
His pestered senses to recoil and start,
When all that is within him does condemn
Itself for being there?

The army of Scottish lords
marches on towards Birnam.

27   **Meet ... weal**: Let's meet the doctor to
this diseased country (i.e. Malcolm)
28   **purge**: cleansing medicine

30   **dew**: water
sovereign: 1 royal; 2 with power as
medicine

Think about

- What two different images
do Caithness and Lennox
use in their final speeches
(lines 25 to 31)? How
effective is each image in
suggesting the parts that
Malcolm and the lords will
have to play in making
Scotland a good country to
live in?

- How do these images link
with (a) others about
Scotland in Act 4; and
(b) images of order and
disorder throughout the
play?

CAITHNESS   Well, march we on,   25
            To give obedience where 'tis truly owed.
            Meet we the medicine of the sickly weal –
            And with him pour we, in our country's purge,
            Each drop of us.

LENNOX   Or so much as it needs
            To dew the sovereign flower and drown the weeds.   30
            Make we our march towards Birnam.

                    Drums beat again. Exeunt, marching.

Act 5 Scene 3

In this scene ...

- In his castle, Macbeth refuses to hear any more reports of the forces facing him, confident that he cannot be harmed.
- The Doctor reports that Lady Macbeth is sick in her mind.
- Macbeth prepares to fight, armed with the Witches' predictions.

Macbeth receives reports of the approaching armies, but takes comfort in the Witches' predictions.

1 **Let ... all**: I don't care if they all desert me
3 **taint**: become weak with

5 **All ... consequences**: everything that will happen to human beings
7 **false**: treacherous

8 **epicures**: people who live soft lives
9 **sway**: rule myself

11 **cream-faced loon**: idiot, white with fear
12 **goose look**: look of a foolish goose

Think about

- What does Macbeth's treatment of his servants reveal about his state of mind?

- Check that you recall the wording of the prophecies which are giving Macbeth confidence here (lines 2 to 7). What effect have those prophecies had on Macbeth's mood here, and his attitude towards the attacking forces?

14 **prick ... fear**: smear your face with blood to cover the paleness
15 **lily-livered**: cowardly
patch: clown / fool
16 **linen**: i.e. bleached white
17 **are ... fear**: persuade others to be afraid
whey-face: white with fear
20 **push**: attack
21 **disseat me**: throw me off my throne

23 **Is ... sere**: has become withered (like a dying plant)
25 **As**: such as

Dunsinane: inside the castle.

Enter MACBETH, *with the* DOCTOR *and attendants.*

MACBETH   Bring me no more reports! Let them fly all!
             Till Birnam wood remove to Dunsinane
             I cannot taint with fear. What's the boy Malcolm?
             Was he not born of woman? The spirits that know
             All mortal consequences have pronounced me thus: 5
             'Fear not, Macbeth: no man that's born of woman
             Shall e'er have power upon thee.' – Then fly, false
                thanes,
             And mingle with the English epicures.
             The mind I sway by, and the heart I bear,
             Shall never sag with doubt, nor shake with fear.   10

Enter a SERVANT.

             The devil damn thee black, thou cream-faced loon!
             Where got'st thou that goose look?

SERVANT   There is ten thousand –

MACBETH   Geese, villain?

SERVANT   Soldiers, sir.

MACBETH   Go, prick thy face and over-red thy fear,
             Thou lily-livered boy. What soldiers, patch?   15
             Death of thy soul! Those linen cheeks of thine
             Are counsellors to fear. What soldiers, whey-face?

SERVANT   The English force, so please you.

MACBETH   Take thy face hence! – (*Exit* SERVANT) – Seyton! – I am
                sick at heart,
             When I behold – Seyton, I say! – This push   20
             Will cheer me ever, or disseat me now.
             I have lived long enough. My way of life
             Is fall'n into the sere, the yellow leaf –
             And that which should accompany old age,
             As honour, love, obedience, troops of friends,   25

Macbeth faces the fact that he
cannot look forward to an old
age of happiness and respect.
The Doctor reports that Lady
Macbeth is sick in her mind.

Think about

- What exactly does Macbeth
seem to be regretting in
lines 22 to 28? Do you feel
any sympathy for him here?

26 **must ... have**: cannot expect
    stead: place
27 **mouth-honour**: flattery
27–8 **breath ... deny**: words which are mere
    air and which the speaker would
    prefer to deny having said

35 **skirr**: scour / raid through

38 **As ... fancies**: rather that she is
    disturbed by persistent hallucinations

40 **minister to**: treat (as a doctor)
42 **Raze out**: erase / rub out
43 **oblivious antidote**: medicine which
    would help her forget
44 **stuffed bosom**: over-full heart
    perilous stuff: dangerous, tormenting
    thoughts
45–6 **Therein ... himself**: That is something
    that the patient has to provide their
    own treatment for
47 **physic**: medicine
48 **staff**: a mace, carried to show that he
    is King
50 **dispatch**: get on with it
50–1 **cast ... land**: analyse the urine (to find
    what disease the patient has)
52 **purge ... health**: cleanse it to its
    original good health

I must not look to have – but in their stead,
Curses, not loud but deep, mouth-honour, breath,
Which the poor heart would fain deny, and dare not.
Seyton!

Enter SEYTON.

SEYTON   What's your gracious pleasure?

MACBETH   What news more?   30

SEYTON   All is confirmed, my lord, which was reported.

MACBETH   I'll fight, till from my bones my flesh be hacked!
Give me my armour.

SEYTON   'Tis not needed yet.

MACBETH   I'll put it on.
Send out more horses, skirr the country round.   35
Hang those that talk of fear. Give me mine armour. –
How does your patient, doctor?

DOCTOR   Not so sick, my lord,
As she is troubled with thick-coming fancies,
That keep her from her rest.

MACBETH   Cure her of that. –
Canst thou not minister to a mind diseased,   40
Pluck from the memory a rooted sorrow,
Raze out the written troubles of the brain,
And with some sweet, oblivious antidote
Cleanse the stuffed bosom of that perilous stuff
Which weighs upon the heart?

DOCTOR   Therein the patient   45
Must minister to himself.

MACBETH   Throw physic to the dogs! I'll none of it. –
(*To* SEYTON) Come, put mine armour on. Give me my
      staff.
Seyton, send out. – Doctor, the thanes fly from me. –
(*To* SEYTON) Come, sir, dispatch! – If thou couldst,
      doctor, cast   50
The water of my land, find her disease,
And purge it to a sound and pristine health,

As Macbeth puts on his armour, the Doctor leaves, wishing he were far away from Dunsinane.

55 rhubarb … drug: laxatives

59 bane: destruction

62 Profit: financial reward

Think about

- What do Macbeth's instructions to Seyton add here? How would the scene be different if it simply showed an uninterrupted exchange between Macbeth and the Doctor?

- In what ways is Macbeth continuing the imagery of medicine used by the lords at the end of Act 5 Scene 2? What is he saying through the imagery in lines 55 to 56?

I would applaud thee to the very echo,
That should applaud again. – (*To* SEYTON) Pull 't off, I
  say! –
(*To the* DOCTOR) What rhubarb, senna, or what
  purgative drug,   55
Would scour these English hence? – Hear'st thou of
  them?

DOCTOR   Ay, my good lord: your royal preparation
Makes us hear something.

MACBETH   (*To* SEYTON) Bring it after me. –
I will not be afraid of death and bane
Till Birnam forest come to Dunsinane.   60

Exit, followed by SEYTON *and attendants.*

DOCTOR   Were I from Dunsinane away and clear,
Profit again should hardly draw me here.

Exit.

In this scene ...

- Malcolm orders every man to cut down and carry a bough from Birnam Wood so that it will be hard to see how big his army is.
- He reports that many men have deserted Macbeth.

2 **chambers**: bedrooms

We ... nothing: We have no doubt of it

4 **hew**: cut
5 **shadow**: conceal
6 **numbers ... host**: size of our army
discovery: people who spy on us
7 **Err ... us**: give mistaken reports about us
8 **We ... but**: All we know is that
9–10 **will ... before 't**: is willing to let us lay siege to it
11 **where ... gone**: whenever they see an opportunity to get away
12 **more and less**: i.e. nobles and common soldiers
13 **constrainèd things**: wretched men forced to fight
14–15 **Let ... event**: i.e. We will only know after the battle whether the reports are true or not
15–16 **put ... soldiership**: behave like efficient soldiers
17 **due decision**: correct assessment
18 **shall say we have**: can claim to have achieved
owe: possess
19 **Thoughts ... relate**: Guesswork builds up our hopes
20 **certain ... arbitrate**: it is the fighting that decides the actual outcome

Think about

- If you were the director, how would you stage in the theatre the moment when the soldiers are ordered to cut down boughs from the trees (lines 4 to 7)?

194

Near Dunsinane: the edge of Birnam forest.

Enter soldiers, with drums beating and banners.

Enter MALCOLM, SIWARD *and his son (*YOUNG SIWARD*),* MACDUFF,

MENTEITH, CAITHNESS, ANGUS, LENNOX, *and* ROSS.

MALCOLM	Cousins, I hope the days are near at hand That chambers will be safe.	
MENTEITH	We doubt it nothing.	
SIWARD	What wood is this before us?	
MENTEITH	The wood of Birnam.	
MALCOLM	Let every soldier hew him down a bough, And bear 't before him. Thereby shall we shadow The numbers of our host, and make discovery Err in report of us.	5
A SOLDIER	It shall be done.	
SIWARD	We learn no other but the confident tyrant Keeps still in Dunsinane, and will endure Our setting down before 't.	
MALCOLM	'Tis his main hope. For where there is advantage to be gone, Both more and less have given him the revolt, And none serve with him but constrainèd things, Whose hearts are absent too.	10
MACDUFF	Let our just censures Attend the true event, and put we on Industrious soldiership.	15
SIWARD	The time approaches That will, with due decision, make us know What we shall say we have, and what we owe. Thoughts speculative their unsure hopes relate, But certain issue strokes must arbitrate – Towards which, advance the war!	20

Drums beat again. Exeunt, marching.

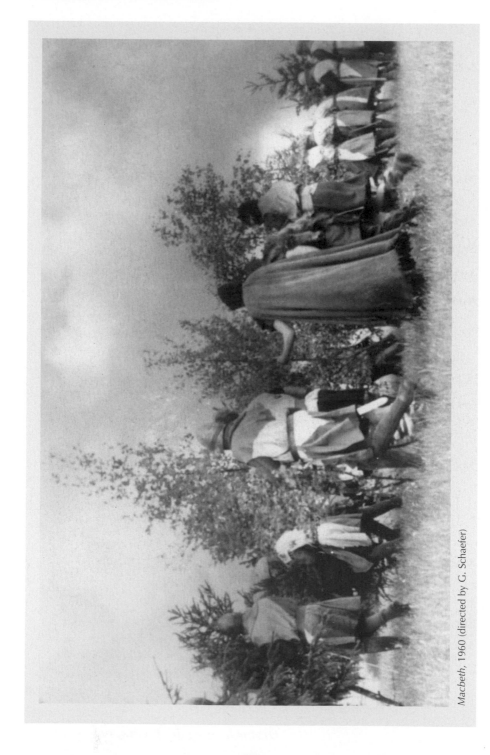

Macbeth, 1960 (directed by G. Schaefer)

Ludlow Festival, 2001

In this scene ...

- Macbeth is told that Lady Macbeth is dead.
- When Birnam Wood begins to move, his earlier confidence in the Witches' prophecies is shaken.
- Macbeth resolves to die fighting.

Boasting that his castle can stand a siege of any length, Macbeth is disturbed by a sudden cry of women. Receiving the news that Lady Macbeth is dead, he thinks about life and death.

4 **famine**: starvation
ague: fever

5 **forced ... ours**: reinforced with people who should be on our side

6 **dareful ... beard**: defiantly in open battle

11 **fell of hair**: hair on my skin

12 **dismal treatise**: frightening story

13 **supped full with**: had my fill of

14 **Direness**: horror
slaughterous thoughts: murderous mind

15 **once start me**: shock me now
Wherefore ... cry: What was that cry about

17 **She ... hereafter**: 1 she ought to have died some time in the future; 2 she would have had to die some time or other

19–21 **Tomorrow ... time**: Each day follows the next, creeping along, until the last word has been written down in the book of time

22–3 **lighted ... death**: provided a light for fools on their journey to the grave

24 **poor player**: 1 unfortunate; 2 incompetent actor

25 **struts and frets**: swaggers and talks agitatedly

Think about

- Line 18 could mean (a) there was a time when I could have responded to such news; (b) the word would have to be spoken at some time; or (c) there would have been a better time for such news. Which of these meanings best fits your interpretation of the play so far?

Dunsinane: inside the castle.

Drums beat a call to arms. Enter Macbeth, Seyton, *and*

soldiers with Macbeth's banner.

MACBETH   Hang out our banners on the outward walls.
          The cry is still, 'They come!' Our castle's strength
          Will laugh a siege to scorn. Here let them lie,
          Till famine and the ague eat them up!
          Were they not forced with those that should be ours,   5
          We might have met them dareful, beard to beard,
          And beat them backward home. (*A sudden sound of
            women's cries is heard.*) What is that noise?

SEYTON   It is the cry of women, my good lord.

                                                        Exit.

MACBETH   I have almost forgot the taste of fears.
          The time has been, my senses would have cooled   10
          To hear a night-shriek; and my fell of hair
          Would, at a dismal treatise, rouse and stir,
          As life were in 't. I have supped full with horrors:
          Direness, familiar to my slaughterous thoughts,
          Cannot once start me.

          Re-enter SEYTON.

                              Wherefore was that cry?   15

SEYTON   The Queen, my lord, is dead.

MACBETH   She should have died hereafter:
          There would have been a time for such a word. –
          Tomorrow, and tomorrow, and tomorrow,
          Creeps in this petty pace from day to day,   20
          To the last syllable of recorded time –
          And all our yesterdays have lighted fools
          The way to dusty death. Out, out, brief candle!
          Life's but a walking shadow, a poor player
          That struts and frets his hour upon the stage,   25

When a messenger reports that Birnam Wood appears to be moving, Macbeth begins to realise that the Witches have deceived him. Now feeling tired of life, he decides to fight to the end.

Think about

- What is Macbeth's view of life conveyed in his soliloquy (speech in which he shares his private thoughts with the audience) in lines 19 to 28? How is it conveyed through images of the theatre?

- In what ways has Macbeth been the victim of 'equivocation' (line 43)?

31 **should**: 1 ought to; 2 want to

34 **anon**: suddenly

36 **endure your wrath**: suffer your anger

38 **grove**: wood

39 **next**: nearest
40 **Till ... thee**: until you shrivel up from starvation
    sooth: truth
42 **pull in resolution**: am beginning to lose my determination
43 **doubt ... fiend**: be suspicious of the devil who tells me one thing and means something else
44 **That ... truth**: which make lies sound like truth
47 **avouches**: claims
48 **nor ... tarrying**: no escape by running away or by staying here
49 **'gin ... sun**: am beginning to be tired of life
50 **th' estate ... undone**: that the universe would fall apart
51 **wrack**: destruction
52 **harness**: armour

And then is heard no more. It is a tale
Told by an idiot, full of sound and fury,
Signifying nothing.

Enter a MESSENGER.

Thou com'st to use thy tongue: thy story, quickly.

MESSENGER   Gracious my lord,   30
I should report that which I say I saw,
But know not how to do it.

MACBETH   Well: say, sir.

MESSENGER   As I did stand my watch upon the hill,
I looked toward Birnam, and anon, methought,
The wood began to move.

MACBETH   Liar and slave!   35

MESSENGER   Let me endure your wrath, if 't be not so.
Within this three mile may you see it coming. –
I say, a moving grove.

MACBETH   If thou speak'st false,
Upon the next tree shalt thou hang alive,
Till famine cling thee! If thy speech be sooth,   40
I care not if thou dost for me as much. –
I pull in resolution, and begin
To doubt th' equivocation of the fiend,
That lies like truth. 'Fear not, till Birnam wood
Do come to Dunsinane' – and now a wood   45
Comes toward Dunsinane. – Arm! Arm, and out! –
If this which he avouches does appear,
There is nor flying hence, nor tarrying here.
I 'gin to be aweary of the sun,
And wish th' estate o' th' world were now undone.   50
Ring the alarum bell! – Blow, wind! Come, wrack!
At least we'll die with harness on our back.

                                                    Exeunt.

Act 5 Scene 6

In this scene ...

- Malcolm instructs Siward and his son to take charge of the leading regiments.
- Malcolm then orders the trumpets to sound.

2 **show ... are**: let the enemy see you as you really are

4 **first battle**: the main part of the army

6 **order**: battle plan

7 **Do we but**: If we can only

10 **clamorous harbingers**: noisy announcers

---**Think about**---

- Think about the staging of Act 5 Scenes 5, 6 and 7. What purposes does the short Scene 6 have?

Dunsinane: open ground outside the castle.

Enter soldiers, with drum and banners. Others carry green

branches from the forest. Enter MALCOLM *and* SIWARD, *with*

MACDUFF.

MALCOLM Now, near enough: your leafy screens throw down,
    And show like those you are. – (*To* SIWARD) You,
     worthy uncle,
    Shall with my cousin, your right noble son,
    Lead our first battle. Worthy Macduff and we
    Shall take upon 's what else remains to do,   5
    According to our order.

SIWARD   Fare you well. –
    Do we but find the tyrant's power tonight,
    Let us be beaten, if we cannot fight.

MACDUFF Make all our trumpets speak! – Give them all breath –
    Those clamorous harbingers of blood and death. 10

Drums beat a call to arms, and trumpets sound. Exeunt.

In this scene ...

- Battle has begun. Macbeth kills Young Siward, but his castle is soon surrendered.
- Macduff searches the battlefield for Macbeth.

Macbeth kills Siward's son, confident that he cannot be harmed by any man born of woman. Macduff is hunting for Macbeth, determined that he should be the one to kill him.

2 **bear-like ... course**: i.e. I have no choice but to fight it out (a reference to bear-baiting with dogs)
What's he: What man exists

10 **abhorrèd**: detested

Think about

- What are Macbeth's feelings and attitudes as the battle begins? Look at Act 5 Scene 5, lines 42 to 44, 49 to 50, and 51 to 52, and Act 5 Scene 7, lines 1 to 4.

- How might Macbeth be affected by the fact that one of the predictions has turned out to be equivocation?

15 **with ... mine**: i.e. if anybody else has killed you
17 **kerns**: Irish foot-soldiers
18 **hired**: i.e. they are paid to fight
staves: spears
Either thou: I will either fight you
19 **unbattered**: undamaged (because he would not have used it)

Battlefield, near the castle gates.

Trumpet calls and noise of fighting.

Enter Macbeth.

MACBETH   They have tied me to a stake: I cannot fly,
               But, bear-like, I must fight the course. – What's he
               That was not born of woman? Such a one
               Am I to fear, or none.

       Enter Young Siward.

YOUNG SIWARD What is thy name?

MACBETH   Thou'lt be afraid to hear it.   5

YOUNG SIWARD No! – though thou call'st thyself a hotter name
               Than any is in hell.

MACBETH   My name's Macbeth.

YOUNG SIWARD The devil himself could not pronounce a title
               More hateful to mine ear.

MACBETH   No, nor more fearful.

YOUNG SIWARD Thou liest, abhorrèd tyrant! With my sword   10
               I'll prove the lie thou speak'st.

       They fight. Young Siward *is killed.*

MACBETH   Thou wast born of woman.
               – But swords I smile at, weapons laugh to scorn,
               Brandished by man that's of a woman born.

                                              Exit.

       Noise of battle continues. Enter Macduff.

MACDUFF   That way the noise is. – Tyrant, show thy face! –
               If thou be'st slain, and with no stroke of mine,   15
               My wife and children's ghosts will haunt me still.
               I cannot strike at wretched kerns, whose arms
               Are hired to bear their staves. Either thou, Macbeth! –
               Or else my sword, with an unbattered edge,

With Macbeth's forces almost defeated, Malcolm and Old Siward victoriously enter the castle.

20 **sheathe**: replace in its sheath
   undeeded: unused
21–2 **By this ... bruited**: i.e. There is so much noise that someone important must be here
23 **And ... not**: That's all I ask

24 **gently rendered**: surrendered without much fighting

27 **The day ... yours**: It is very nearly possible to declare the victory yours

28–9 **foes ... us**: soldiers in Macbeth's army who 1 fight on our side; or 2 deliberately strike so as to miss us

Think about

• What problems might be encountered in staging the fight sequences in Act 5 Scene 7? Think about, for example, what you would do with Young Siward's body, as his father does not see it when he enters.

• What are the dramatic effects of having the scene constantly switching from Dunsinane to the surrounding countryside in this Act?

I sheathe again undeeded. There thou shouldst be!   **20**
By this great clatter, one of greatest note
Seems bruited. Let me find him, Fortune! –
And more I beg not.

Exit. Battle-noise continues.

Enter MALCOLM, *with* SIWARD.

SIWARD
This way, my lord! – The castle's gently rendered.
The tyrant's people on both sides do fight;   **25**
The noble thanes do bravely in the war. –
The day almost itself professes yours,
And little is to do.

MALCOLM
We have met with foes
That strike beside us.

SIWARD
Enter, sir, the castle.

Exeunt. Trumpet calls: battle-noise continues.

In this scene ...

• Macbeth finally encounters Macduff, and is killed.

Macbeth finally faces Macduff, who destroys Macbeth's confidence by revealing that he was not born of a woman in the usual way, but by a Caesarean operation. Shocked by this news, Macbeth at first refuses to fight him.

1–2 play ... sword: i.e. commit suicide as defeated Roman soldiers sometimes did

2 lives: living enemies
gashes: wounds

4 Of all men else: More than all other men

5 charged: weighed down

6 blood of thine: your family's blood

8 Than ... out: than words can say
Thou ... labour: You're wasting your efforts

9 intrenchant: uncuttable

10 keen: sharp
impress: cut

11 vulnerable crests: helmets of men who can be wounded

13 Despair thy charm: Give up the hope offered by the magic spell

14 angel: evil spirit

16 Untimely ripped: i.e. delivered prematurely, by a Caesarean operation

18 cowed ... man: disheartened me

19 juggling: deceiving

20 palter ... sense: cheat us with double meanings

21–2 That ... hope: who sound as though they are keeping their word, but then dash our hopes

— **Think about** —

• What are Macbeth's thoughts at this point about (a) life and death (lines 1 to 3); and (b) fighting Macduff (lines 4 to 6)?

• What do you think Macbeth now feels about the Witches and their predictions?

The battlefield.

Enter MACBETH.

MACBETH	Why should I play the Roman fool, and die On mine own sword? Whiles I see lives, the gashes Do better upon them!

Enter MACDUFF.

MACDUFF	Turn, hell-hound! Turn!
MACBETH	Of all men else I have avoided thee. – But get thee back, my soul is too much charged 5 With blood of thine already.
MACDUFF	I have no words: My voice is in my sword – thou bloodier villain Than terms can give thee out!

They fight.

MACBETH	Thou losest labour, As easy may'st thou the intrenchant air With thy keen sword impress, as make me bleed. 10 Let fall thy blade on vulnerable crests: I bear a charmèd life, which must not yield To one of woman born.
MACDUFF	Despair thy charm! – And let the angel whom thou still hast served Tell thee: Macduff was from his mother's womb 15 Untimely ripped.
MACBETH	Accursèd be that tongue that tells me so! – For it hath cowed my better part of man. And be these juggling fiends no more believed That palter with us in a double sense – 20 That keep the word of promise to our ear, And break it to our hope! – I'll not fight with thee.

Rather than surrender to
Malcolm, Macbeth continues to
fight and is killed by Macduff.

24 **show ... time**: a famous public
spectacle
25 **monsters**: strange creatures
26 **Painted upon a pole**: i.e. Macbeth's
picture will be hung up
underwrit: with writing underneath

29 **baited ... curse**: taunted and cursed by
the mob
31 **thou opposed being**: even if you, the
man fighting me, are
32 **try the last**: fight to the end
33 **Lay on**: Come on, start fighting again
34 **Hold, enough**: Stop, I give in

Think about

• In some productions
Macbeth and Macduff go
off fighting and Macbeth is
killed off-stage. His severed
head is then brought on in
Act 5 Scene 9. If you were
the director, would you
have killed Macbeth
on-stage or off? Would you
make the same decision in
a film?

MACDUFF   Then yield thee, coward –
                         And live to be the show and gaze o' th' time.
                         We'll have thee, as our rarer monsters are,   25
                         Painted upon a pole, and underwrit,
                         'Here may you see the tyrant'.

MACBETH   I will not yield
                         To kiss the ground before young Malcolm's feet,
                         And to be baited with the rabble's curse.
                         Though Birnam wood be come to Dunsinane,   30
                         And thou opposed being of no woman born –
                         Yet I will try the last. Before my body
                         I throw my warlike shield. Lay on, Macduff! –
                         And damned be him that first cries 'Hold, enough!'

Exeunt, fighting on. Noise of battle comes to a climax, then fades. They re-enter still fighting, and MACBETH *is killed.*

Exit MACDUFF, *dragging away the body.*

In this scene ...

- Malcolm and his supporters are victorious. He rewards the lords and invites them to his coronation.

Siward expresses pride that his son died bravely.

1 **I would**: I wish

2 **must go off**: have to die

3 **So ... bought**: i.e. we have won a great victory with little loss of life

5 **a soldier's debt**: i.e. he paid with his life

7 **The which ... confirmed**: and no sooner had he confirmed his manhood by his bravery

8 **the ... fought**: the front of the fighting from which he didn't retreat

12 **before**: on the front of his body

14 **hairs**: wordplay on 'hairs' and 'heirs'

16 **knell is knolled**: funeral bell has tolled

Think about

- What do you think about Siward's reaction to his son's death? Does it seem hard-hearted, for example? Or is it the way soldiers might have reacted in Shakespeare's time?

18 **parted well**: died well
paid his score: settled his account

19 **newer comfort**: better, more comforting news

Dunsinane: in the castle courtyard.

Trumpet fanfare. Enter MALCOLM *and* SIWARD, *with* ROSS,

LENNOX, MENTEITH, CAITHNESS, *and* ANGUS. *Soldiers follow, with*

drum and banners.

MALCOLM	I would the friends we miss were safe arrived.
SIWARD	Some must go off. And yet, by these I see,
	So great a day as this is cheaply bought.
MALCOLM	Macduff is missing, and your noble son.
ROSS	Your son, my lord, has paid a soldier's debt.

5

He only lived but till he was a man –
The which no sooner had his prowess confirmed
In the unshrinking station where he fought,
But like a man he died.

SIWARD   Then he is dead?

ROSS   Ay, and brought off the field. Your cause of sorrow   10
Must not be measured by his worth, for then
It hath no end.

SIWARD   Had he his hurts before?

ROSS   Ay, on the front.

SIWARD   Why then, God's soldier be he!
Had I as many sons as I have hairs,
I would not wish them to a fairer death.   15
And so, his knell is knolled.

MALCOLM   He's worth more sorrow,
And that I'll spend for him.

SIWARD   He's worth no more.
They say he parted well, and paid his score:
And so, God be with him! – Here comes newer
    comfort.

Macduff enters with Macbeth's severed head. Malcolm rewards the loyal lords by giving each of them the new title of earl. He invites everyone to his coronation at Scone.

Think about

- Malcolm's final speech seems to suggest that all will now be well, but modern productions often take a different line. If you were the director, how might you show each of the following very different interpretations in the final moments of the play: (a) that there will now be peace and happiness in Scotland; (b) that Malcolm will not be strong enough to prevent civil war from breaking out; (c) that Malcolm will himself prove to be a tyrant; and (d) that Fleance is waiting to take over, as the Witches prophesied he would?

---

21 **usurper**: someone who forces a rightful king off his throne and takes his place
The time: The world (our time and country)

22 **compassed … pearl**: surrounded by your kingdom's finest noblemen

23 **That … minds**: i.e. I am speaking their thoughts

27 **reckon … loves**: reward you individually for your love and loyalty

28 **make … you**: so that I'm no longer in debt to you

29 **Henceforth**: from this time onwards

31 **Which … time**: which ought to be given a new start in this new era

32 **As**: such as

33 **watchful tyranny**: i.e. Macbeth's spies

34 **Producing forth**: bringing out of hiding
ministers: agents

36–7 **by … life**: killed herself violently

37–8 **needful … us**: other necessary matters demand my attention

38 **by … Grace**: with God's help

39 **measure … place:** the proper order, at the right time and place

Enter MACDUFF, *with* MACBETH's *head on a pole.*

MACDUFF   (*To* MALCOLM) Hail, King! – for so thou art. Behold
                    where stands   20
                    Th' usurper's cursèd head. The time is free!
                    I see thee compassed with thy kingdom's pearl,
                    That speak my salutation in their minds –
                    Whose voices I desire aloud with mine. –
                    Hail, King of Scotland!

ALL   Hail, King of Scotland!   25

Trumpet fanfare.

MALCOLM   We shall not spend a large expense of time
                    Before we reckon with your several loves,
                    And make us even with you. My thanes and kinsmen,
                    Henceforth be earls, the first that ever Scotland
                    In such an honour named. What's more to do,   30
                    Which would be planted newly with the time, –
                    As calling home our exiled friends abroad
                    That fled the snares of watchful tyranny;
                    Producing forth the cruel ministers
                    Of this dead butcher and his fiend-like queen,   35
                    Who, as 'tis thought, by self and violent hands
                    Took off her life; – this, and what needful else
                    That calls upon us, by the grace of Grace,
                    We will perform in measure, time and place.
                    So thanks to all at once, and to each one –   40
                    Whom we invite to see us crowned at Scone.

                              Trumpets sound again. Exeunt.

Birmingham Repertory Theatre, 1995

National Theatre, 1972

RSC, 1982

RSC, 1982

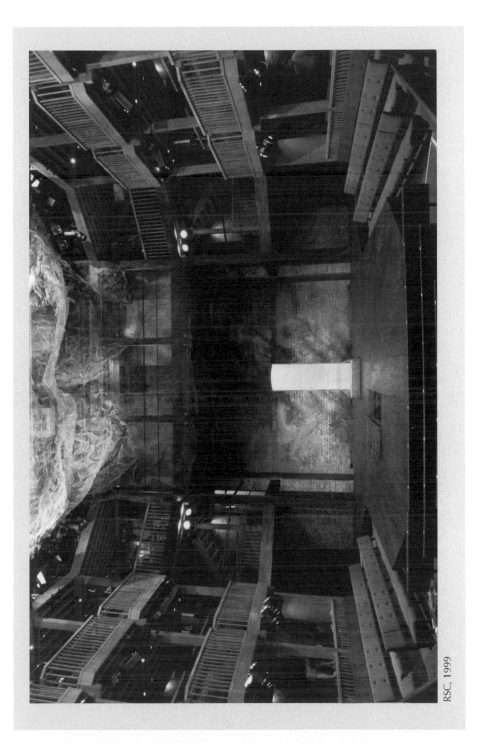

RSC, 1999

Macbeth was first performed in 1606 and it is a play that very much reflects the issues and events of the time it was written. In particular, it seems to have been written with a specific king in mind. In 1603 King James VI of Scotland succeeded Queen Elizabeth I. He became King James I of England and was the first monarch of both Scotland and England. He is a focus of the play in a number of ways.

SCOTLAND AND JAMES' ANCESTORS

Macbeth is set in Scotland and many of the characters in the play are James' ancestors. In Shakespeare's play the actions of Banquo, James' ancestor, are contrasted with the murderous Macbeth's. Both hear the Witches' prophecies but they react in very different ways.

When Malcolm creates Scotland's first earls at the end of the play, audiences would have been reminded of James's own generosity when he became King in handing out honours and titles.

KINGSHIP AND LOYALTY

Macbeth explores the importance of kingship and loyalty. In Shakespeare's England the king was widely believed to be God's representative on Earth, at the head of the 'natural' order. To murder a king was therefore the ultimate crime – one that could have only 'unnatural' results. When Macbeth murders Duncan, the natural world is immediately turned upside-down. The sun does not rise and Duncan's horses eat each other. Such events continue throughout the play and it is clear how serious the consequences of killing a king are.

THE GUNPOWDER PLOT

Some of the themes and issues in *Macbeth* are related to the Gunpowder Plot – the attempt in 1605 to blow up the King (James I) and Parliament (the government). In the trials that followed, a conspirator called Father Garnet became notorious for 'equivocating' (telling half-truths). *Macbeth* was written in the same year as Garnet's trial and as a result has a lot to say about equivocation. The Witches constantly tell Macbeth half-truths, and the Porter admits an imaginary equivocator to hell.

WITCHCRAFT

The Witches play a significant part in *Macbeth* and this would have interested James I. He was an expert on witchcraft, having written a book on the subject called *Demonologie*. The book described witches' powers of predicting the future, defying normal physical laws, affecting the weather, cursing their enemies, using 'familiar' spirits in the shape of animals, and taking demonic possession of innocent people. Shakespeare's Weird Sisters do many of these things.

While James was still King of Scotland, over 300 people accused of being witches were tortured to make them confess that they were conspiring against the King. James sometimes took part in the trials himself. In Elizabeth's England, hundreds of people (nearly all women) had been executed as witches.

In Shakespeare's time, people might have seen witchcraft and its effects in the world around them – a sickly child, a failed crop, a lost business deal. They would also have recognised the signs of someone possessed by demons – a trance-like state, actions that were out of character, hallucinations, and the inability to sleep. All of these they would see in the character of Macbeth.

Macbeth was written for performance in the Globe playhouse, the famous theatre on the south bank of the river Thames in London in which Shakespeare's acting company, the King's Men, was based.

What we know about the staging of plays in the Globe four hundred years ago comes mainly from the evidence of plays, like *Macbeth*, that we know were performed there. Sometimes other evidence helps, such as theatre-builders' contracts, lists of expensive costumes and props, or, less commonly, eye-witness accounts of visits to the theatre in Shakespeare's time. One such audience member, who saw *Macbeth* in 1611, records being impressed by the Witches, who would have been played by men in Shakespeare's time. And he was even more impressed by Act 3 Scene 4 where the ghost of the murdered Banquo interrupts Macbeth's royal feast. When Macbeth stood to drink to Banquo, the ghost 'came and sat down in his chair behind him.' And when Macbeth turned to sit, the blood-stained ghost glared up at him, and Macbeth 'fell into a great passion of fear and fury…'.

Banquo's ghost may have had some distance to move, eerily, when it 'disappeared'. The stage of the Globe was big (about 13 metres wide by 9 metres deep), and the action on it would have been continuous, with no intervals between Acts or scenes. No scenery or stage-lighting, as we think of them, was used. The play's language would have been enough to suggest places and settings to the imagination of its audience. Burning torches, often used in *Macbeth*, were not for lighting, but to tell the audience, in the open-air afternoon daylight of the Globe, that it was watching a 'night-time' scene. When Duncan approaches Macbeth's castle in Act 1 Scene 6, the 'castle' would have been only the decorated rising wall of the dressing-room at the back of the stage, with its two main entrances. Costumes, such as indoor or outdoor dress, armour or casual clothing, would also have signalled different settings and kinds of character for spectators.

When the murderers attack Banquo and Fleance in Act 3 Scene 3, they may well have hidden behind the two great oak pillars which supported the canopy over the stage known as 'the heavens'. And when the Witches' cauldron sinks from sight after producing its 'apparitions' in Act 4 Scene 1, it would have descended through the main trap-door in the stage into the hidden under-stage area, known as 'hell'. The stage itself, between 'heaven' and 'hell', represented our world as a kind of 'middle-earth'.

Actors on the stage, especially comic characters or specialist clowns, might sometimes play directly with spectators in the yard. The Porter in Act 2 Scene 3 of *Macbeth*, for example, might have picked on particular spectators with his invitations to 'Hell' – and when he departs saying, 'I pray you, remember the Porter', he was probably asking not just for a tip, but for applause for his hungover, drunken comic routine.

Staging in Shakespeare's theatre may seem crude or simple by modern standards, but it was in fact very flexible and effective in playing to the imaginations of its audiences. The 'special effects' in *Macbeth*, which included a frighteningly visible blood-spattered ghost and apparitions rising out of 'hell' through a cauldron, were impressively 'state of the art' for their time. And those who saw them in the Globe were prepared to use their imaginations to engage with the language, fears and dangers of the play.

A play in performance at the reconstruction of Shakespeare's Globe

As with all of Shakespeare's plays, there is no single 'correct meaning' of *Macbeth*. Different people interpret it in different ways, and new meanings are found every time it is performed. But there are some basic questions that any director of this play has to address. Three of the most important are:

- When the play begins is Macbeth already a bad man who provides a ready source of evil for the Witches to tap into? Or is he just a weak-willed man, who is manipulated by the Witches?
- As the play ends is Scotland likely to have a free and happy time under King Malcolm? Or can it expect further troubles?
- What time and place should the play be set in to get the chosen interpretation across to the audience?

MACBETH AND THE WITCHES
Many directors have taken the view that it is the Witches who are in control, luring Macbeth to evil for their own ends. This can make very exciting and dramatic theatre, and is the interpretation taken by three major productions (all available on video). Two are films made for cinema, directed by Orson Welles (1948) and Roman Polanski (1971). The third is Gregory Doran's 1999 RSC production.

Orson Welles makes it clear from the opening shots of his 1948 film that the Witches are in charge. As they chant 'Fair is foul ...', they make a hideous clay doll of Macbeth and, at the moment that Macduff kills Macbeth in Act 5 Scene 8, the film cuts to a shot of the doll having its head sliced off. To underline that the Witches have been in control throughout, the final scene is a long shot of Macbeth's castle. As the camera pulls back, the Witches come into view, gazing at the distant castle. Their final words are 'Peace! – the charm's wound up', a line borrowed from Act 1 Scene 3.

Roman Polanski takes a similar approach. His 1971 film opens on a deserted beach where the Witches are burying a severed hand holding a dagger. They depart and the place where they have cast their spell becomes the scene for the battle in which Macbeth and Banquo defeat the rebels. As soon as Macbeth meets the Witches, he seems to come under their spell. When he returns to them in Act 4, he willingly drinks the potion they have brewed for him.

When **Gregory Doran**'s 1999 RSC production (pages 77, 221) was filmed for television, the disruptive power of the Witches could be seen in the fact that they caused interference on the cameras. The opening scene was filmed in a strange green light and the picture looked as though it had not been properly tuned in.

However **Trevor Nunn**'s 1976 RSC production (page 39, also available on video) took a slightly different view. It opened by showing how powerful the Witches were as a force of evil opposing good: Duncan and his men were trying to pray, but their words were drowned out by a terrible howling from the Witches. Macbeth, though, was shown as a man whose problems were deep inside his mind and, although the Witches had some control over him, as they always do, you felt that the evil was more within the man himself. For example, at the point where Banquo's ghost appears in Act 3 Scene 4, Macbeth simply stared, shaking in horror, at an empty space. There was nobody sitting there, but the audience knew exactly what it was that he could see. This interpretation was helped by making the character of Lady Macbeth a powerful and terrifying figure who seemed to have at least as much control over Macbeth as the Witches did.

Macbeth, 1971 (directed by R. Polanski)

THE ENDING

When we read Malcolm's final speech in the text, the most obvious interpretation of the ending is that all will now be well. Scotland seems to have a good, strong King who is starting his reign sensibly by rewarding the nobles who have supported him. **Orson Welles's** 1948 film follows this interpretation with a powerful Malcolm cheered enthusiastically by his new earls. However, many directors in recent years have taken a different view of the ending. **Trevor Nunn's** 1976 RSC production, for example, ended with Malcolm and Macduff sitting in silence, worn out and shocked by the horrors they had been involved in. Their stunned reactions made the audience feel that, though Malcolm would be a good king, the evil would take a long time to wash away.

Polanski took a more dramatic view of the ending. His 1971 film ended with a shot of a single horseman riding across the moors to Malcolm's coronation. Suddenly the rider reigns in his horse. He has heard strange, unearthly musical sounds which we have come to associate with the Witches. He dismounts, and as he descends the rocky hillside to find the Witches, we realise that the horseman is Donalbain, Malcolm's brother. The cycle of killing and evil is about to start all over again.

Gregory Doran's 1999 RSC production seemed to have ended with Malcolm's speech. But suddenly the audience was aware of a strange noise, and at one side of the stage they saw the young Fleance, watching intently and rattling the magic token that the Witches had earlier given to Macbeth. Clearly Fleance was now in the Witches' power and would plot to overthrow Malcolm. This interpretation fits Shakespeare's script well as Banquo is told by the Witches in Act 1 Scene 3 that he will be father to a line of kings. Shakespeare doesn't tell us how that prediction comes true, but some directors take the view that Fleance will now have to overthrow Malcolm. **Dominic Cooke's** 2004 RSC production (pages 63, 182) ended with everyone leaving the stage except Fleance. As he stood there, deep in thought, the Witches crawled out of the darkness towards him.

THE SETTING

A director has to think carefully about when and where to set a production of *Macbeth*. Should the play be set in Shakespeare's own time, for example, with the actors dressed in Jacobean costume? Should it be in modern dress, or possibly set in a period between Shakespeare's time and our own? Recent productions have been set in times and places ranging from the eleventh century, when the historical Macbeth lived, to the modern day, and in places as different as eighteenth century Scotland and medieval Japan.

A modern setting has the obvious attraction that it can speak directly to today's audience. Modern-setting productions often include topical visual jokes. The 1995 **Birmingham Repertory Theatre** production (pages 90 and 216) included a Porter who appeared reading a TV listings magazine with a front-cover photograph of Hugh Grant. The Porter's humour is often difficult to get across to today's audience and a modern setting can make the character and his jokes easier to understand.

The 1972 **National Theatre** production (pages 10, 127, 148, 149, 182, 217) took a very different approach and set the play in Shakespeare's own time. One scene even had traitors' heads stuck on poles (page 217). This setting helped the audience to understand what it might have been like to see a story about killing a king acted in public less than a year after James I himself had narrowly escaped being assassinated by the Gunpowder Plot.

The activities in this section focus on different scenes in the play. The type of activities used can easily be adapted to focus on other sections of the play if necessary. Before beginning the activities you will need to have read the relevant scene.

ACT 1 SCENE 3: MACBETH MEETS THE WITCHES

Each activity in this section leads directly onto the next. However, it is possible to use any of them separately. The focus of the activities is on the nature of the Witches and the different responses to them from Macbeth and Banquo.

THE WITCHES WIND UP THE SPELL

1 Read lines 1 to 38. The First Witch is planning her revenge on a sailor whose wife refused to give her chestnuts. In your own words write an account of what the First Witch plans to do to the sailor.

2 Many people were afraid of witchcraft in England at the time *Macbeth* was written. How would you portray the Witches, if you were staging a production of the play, to highlight their sinister nature? Consider:

- How would they look? What costumes would they wear?
- How would they move about the stage?
- Would the three be very similar to each other or would they each have individual qualities and look different?
- Would you use any theatrical devices to highlight the sinister atmosphere, for example, lighting or sound effects?

3 a The Witches have a strange and powerful way of speaking. In groups of three read lines 33 to 38 aloud together.

   b The verse form that Shakespeare uses here is strong and punchy, capturing the quality of a spell, or a curse. Make up a 'spell' that the Witches could chant just before the appearance of Macbeth. Try to use the same verse form, four heavy beats to a line, and include the number three, used as a 'magic' number in the play.
   Example
   The weird sisters, one, two, three,
   Call on powers from land and sea,
   Drain the blood from pilot's thumb
   To make the noble soldier come!

CAPTURING THE KEY MOMENT OF THE SCENE

1 a In groups of seven, each take one of the following characters: Macbeth, Banquo, First Witch, Second Witch, Third Witch, Ross, and a reporter. Create a space to be the heath on which the meeting with the Witches takes place.

  b Macbeth and Banquo should come to the centre of the heath. Remember this is a wild environment with a violent storm blowing. The reporter should ask Macbeth and Banquo questions about the battle they have just fought.
  Examples
  Macbeth, is it true that you ripped the traitor Macdonwald from the stomach to the mouth?
  Banquo, I believe you have been fighting for three days. How do you feel?

  c The Witches should enter the heath and surround Macbeth and Banquo. The reporter should ask questions to find out from Macbeth what he is thinking and feeling. Macbeth should answer the reporter's questions.
  Example
  Macbeth, what do you think of these strange creatures? How do you think they appeared out of thin air?

  d In turn the Witches should give their greetings to Macbeth (lines 49 to 51). After each greeting the reporter should ask Macbeth how he feels about what they have said to him.
  Example
  Macbeth, how do you feel about the fact that the Witches know who you are?

  e Ross should enter and give Macbeth his urgent message from the King. You can use either the words from the text (lines 90 to 108) or your own words. The reporter should then ask Macbeth how he feels about what he has heard.
  Example
  Congratulations Macbeth. So the Second Witch was right. How do you feel now about the prophecy from the Third Witch?

  f As a group discuss the importance of the message from Ross. Is it from this moment that Macbeth seriously begins to consider the prospect of being King?

The different responses to the Witches from Macbeth and Banquo

1   In pairs read through the scene from the entrance of Macbeth (line 38). As you read, answer the questions below. One person should focus on the response of Macbeth, the other on the response of Banquo.

- How does Macbeth react to the Witches and their prophecies?
- How does Banquo react to the Witches and their prophecies?
- What is Macbeth's state of mind after Ross gives the news that he is Thane of Cawdor?
- What is Banquo's state of mind after Ross gives the news that Macbeth is Thane of Cawdor?

Example
Macbeth hardly speaks. Banquo says that Macbeth 'seems rapt', in a trance. When Macbeth does finally ask the Witches a question, they vanish.

2   a   While Banquo is talking to Ross and Angus, Macbeth speaks and seems almost possessed. In pairs read lines 135 to 138:

MACBETH   If good, why do I yield to that suggestion
             Whose horrid image doth unfix my hair,
             And make my seated heart knock at my ribs
             Against the use of nature?

b   Discuss the following questions:

- What do you think Macbeth is imagining? Is it the murder of Duncan?
- Once Macbeth has 'conjured' this image into his mind, do you think he can ever get rid of it?
- Does the image spring from his imagination or do you think the Witches have placed it there?

3 The following speeches, from lines 119 to 121, and 124 to 127, clearly show different reactions from Macbeth and Banquo.

> **MACBETH** (*To* BANQUO) Do you not hope your children shall be kings,
> When those that gave the Thane of Cawdor to me
> Promised no less to them?
>
> **BANQUO** ... oftentimes, to win us to our harm,
> The instruments of darkness tell us truths,
> Win us with honest trifles, to betray 's
> In deepest consequence.

a In pairs, taking a character each, read these speeches.

b Write a reply that Macbeth could make after Banquo's warning. Remember that the Witches have intended to trick Macbeth, not Banquo. They were there to 'charm' Macbeth. Perhaps if they had wanted to charm Banquo too they could have done so. Consider:

- Why is it, do you think, that Macbeth does not listen to Banquo's warning?
- Is Macbeth under the spell of the Witches, or has their prophesy connected with his own ambition?

ACT 1 SCENE 7: MACBETH AND LADY MACBETH

Each activity in this section leads directly onto the next. However, it is possible to use any of them separately. The focus of the activities is on the relationship between Macbeth and Lady Macbeth.

MACBETH'S SOLILOQUY

Macbeth has had a picture of the murder of Duncan in his mind since meeting the Witches in Act 1 Scene 3: the 'horrid image' that makes his hair stand on end and his heart knock at his ribs. Parts **a** and **c** of the first activity look at this picture, before exploring Macbeth's soliloquy.

1 **a** In pairs decide exactly what this picture might be. How is Macbeth imagining killing Duncan? What makes it so terrifying?

   b Think of three words and an action that create an image of the murder as you have imagined that Macbeth is seeing it.
Example
Your words might be 'hand', 'suffocate' and 'gasp' if you have imagined Macbeth putting his hand over Duncan's mouth to stop him calling out.

   c With your partner discuss the effect such an image might have on Macbeth. Consider:

- How is the violence different from the violence he used when encountering enemies on the battlefield?
- Do you think that such an image, once created by the imagination, can ever entirely disappear?

   d One of you should be Macbeth and quietly read the speech from line 1 to 28. At the same time, the second person should speak the three words or do the action you thought of in part **b**, creating the impression of Macbeth being plagued by his own thoughts. The second person could, for example, move around Macbeth, taunting him.

   e The person playing Macbeth should describe the experience, talking through the pictures that came into their mind when the other person spoke the chosen words. How does it feel when you are unable to push an image from your mind?

2 a Macbeth never calls what he is going to do a murder, but refers to it indirectly several times, e.g. 'th' assassination' and 'his surcease'. In pairs make a list of all the euphemisms (indirect expressions) he uses for the killing.

b With your partner discuss why Macbeth might prefer to call the murder by these other names.

3 a In pairs go through the speech (lines 1 to 28) and make a list of all the arguments against killing Duncan that Macbeth uses, for example, that he is Duncan's host.

b One of you should be Macbeth and read the speech out loud. The second person should act as Macbeth's conscience. Using the list you have made the 'conscience' should call out the reasons why Macbeth must not kill the King at appropriate points in the speech.
Example
The conscience might call out 'Family' when Macbeth says 'First, as I am his kinsman'.

c Write a summing-up speech which the 'conscience' could deliver. It should summarise the reasons why Macbeth should not go ahead with the murder of Duncan. It could begin 'To conclude, the reasons you should not proceed with the plan to kill Duncan are …'.

LADY MACBETH'S TACTICS

There are many different ways of staging this scene. In some productions Lady Macbeth's speeches are delivered as a violent outburst meant to scare Macbeth, but in others she is trying to seduce him and to make him believe that she will find him more attractive if he has the courage to murder Duncan. Occasionally she is played as a woman who is heart-broken, upset because Macbeth is not the man she thought he was. In most productions Lady Macbeth uses a variety of tactics to try to get Macbeth to agree to murder Duncan.

1 a In pairs list five tactics Lady Macbeth uses during this scene. Write out the tactic and a line which illustrates it.
Example
She taunts Macbeth's lack of courage.
'Art thou afeard / To be the same in thine own act and valour, / As thou art in desire?'

b Decide on a physical movement for each of these lines. For example, Lady Macbeth could wag her finger at Macbeth when she is taunting him.

c Think of a physical movement Macbeth could make in response to each line. For example, after the taunting line Macbeth could turn away from Lady Macbeth, or he could catch hold of her as if he is going to hit her.

d Put these five lines and movements together in order to form a shortened version of the scene. Act out this shortened scene.

e How much do you think the words (and actions) of Lady Macbeth affect Macbeth? For example, do they hurt him? Write a line voicing what Macbeth is thinking to follow each of Lady Macbeth's lines.
Example
Lady Macbeth: Art thou afeard / To be the same in thine own act and valour, / As thou art in desire?
Macbeth: Yes, yes I'm scared. For the first time in my life I'm so scared I feel sick.

MACBETH'S SILENCE

At no point in this scene does Macbeth make a real effort to make Lady Macbeth understand why he does not want to murder Duncan. He never manages to voice the arguments that were in his mind just before she entered. The closest he comes is the lines:

> MACBETH I dare do all that may become a man;
> Who dares do more is none.

1 Make a list of the reasons Macbeth might not speak his mind to Lady Macbeth during this scene.
Example
He knows she won't understand.
He wants to be talked into doing the deed.

ACT 2 SCENE 2: THE DEED IS DONE

Each activity in this section leads directly onto the next. However, it is possible to use any of them separately. The focus of the activities is Macbeth's state of mind and the atmosphere created by this scene.

THE KILLING OF DUNCAN

Shakespeare does not show us the moment of Duncan's death, although directors sometimes do show it in some way. In either case it is important to consider the murder in order to understand Macbeth's state of mind at this point of the play.

1 a In pairs write an account for a narrator to read as a voice-over telling the story of the murder up to the moment when Macbeth leaves the chamber having killed the King, the daggers still in his hand. Try to concentrate on creating the tension of the scene.
   Example
   Narrator: Macbeth silently opened the chamber door and stepped into the room. He lit a candle, and moved it to the right then left, in order to see around the room. In the centre was the sleeping Duncan. To Duncan's left were the attendants, drugged ...

   b One person should read out the account you have written and the other should mime the part of Macbeth. Alternatively you could work with another pair and they could play the sleeping attendant and Duncan. At key moments the narrator should clap. When this happens Macbeth should speak his thoughts.

   c Decide at which points other people's words might be going through Macbeth's mind. For example, as he enters the chamber he might hear Lady Macbeth taunting him. Add in these lines, either spoken by the narrator or by an additional actor.

   d Write a second section for the narrator to read based on Macbeth's account in Act 2 Scene 2 of his journey from Duncan's chamber after the deed up to the moment when he returns to Lady Macbeth.
   Example
   Narrator: Macbeth heard a sound as he passed the second chamber. He pressed himself to the keyhole and watched two sleepers wake and pray. Macbeth tried to bless himself but could not say 'Amen.' He sank to his knees, trying to pray. Suddenly he heard a voice cry 'Sleep no more.' He sprang to his feet ...

2 Imagine that you are a director. How could you show Duncan's murder either as a stage scene, or as a film projected while Lady Macbeth is waiting for her husband at the beginning of this scene? Consider:

- What lighting and sound effects would you use?
- What would the key moments be in terms of creating tension in your scene or film?
- What effect would you want this to have on the audience? How would you want to influence their feelings about the character of Macbeth?

3 A few directors of the play have chosen to have the Witches present throughout this scene, for example pushing Macbeth into Duncan's chamber when he hesitated by the door. How else could a director use the Witches in this scene? What effect would including the Witches have on an audience? Consider how it might affect their feelings about Macbeth, for example.

LADY MACBETH AND THE SLEEPING DUNCAN

1 At the beginning of this scene Lady Macbeth says that she would have killed the sleeping Duncan herself if he had not looked like her father. Consider:

- What does this tell us about Lady Macbeth and her emotions at this point in the play?
- Lady Macbeth is often thought of as entirely evil, but does the fact that she could not go through with the murder change your view of her?

2 a Imagine exactly what Lady Macbeth did in Duncan's chamber. She checked on the drugged attendants, laid out the daggers, and looked at the sleeping King. Think about everything she saw, heard and touched, and every emotion she felt.

b In your own words tell the story as if you were Lady Macbeth. Describe everything in as much detail as possible.
Example
I entered the chamber and lit my candle. The guards had drunk from the flask I had given them earlier and were lying sleeping on the floor. One still clutched the flask to his chest and was snoring heavily ...

TWO REALITIES

Throughout this scene Lady Macbeth seems to be practical. She is either not able or does not allow herself to concentrate on whatever fear affected her in Duncan's room. Her only spoken concern or fear is that their crime will be found out. Macbeth's anxieties seem to be very different; he is concerned with the inner or spiritual world, from which he knows he has excluded himself forever. After the murder it seems that he and Lady Macbeth are left trying to communicate from two almost opposing mental and emotional states.

1 a In pairs or small groups go through this scene and find six examples of lines that show that Lady Macbeth's concerns are rooted in the material world, and six examples that show that Macbeth is more concerned with the spiritual.
Example
Lady Macbeth: A little water clears us of this deed.
Macbeth: Will all great Neptune's ocean wash this blood / Clean from this hand?

b Discuss why you think there is this difference between Macbeth and Lady Macbeth. For example, does Macbeth have a greater imagination and ability to see the bigger picture and the consequences? Or does Lady Macbeth know that if she allows herself to dwell on the fear she will be unable to cope?

2 Macbeth expresses crippling regret at the end of this scene when he says, 'Wake Duncan with thy knocking! I would thou couldst!' Consider:

- Do you think Lady Macbeth could ever have understood this remorse, at this point in the play?
- What might her response have been, do you think, if he had tried to talk to her about it at this point?
- What do the audience expect the effect on Macbeth will be if he has no-one he can talk to about the way he is feeling?

ACT 3 SCENE 4: THE BANQUET

Each activity in this section leads directly onto the next. However, it is possible to use any of them separately. The focus of the activities is the staging of the banquet and the effect of Macbeth's behaviour.

STAGING THE SCENE

1   There are six 'sections' to the scene, listed below. In pairs write a shortened version of the scene with two to four lines for each section. The lines can either be Shakespeare's language taken from the scene, or your own words.

- The Macbeths welcoming the guests
- Macbeth speaking to the murderer
- The first appearance of Banquo's ghost
- The second appearance of Banquo's ghost
- Lady Macbeth ushering the guests out
- Macbeth and Lady Macbeth alone

2   Table scenes are often difficult to stage as they do not involve much movement. In this scene there is the added complication of who must be able to hear what, and when. For example the audience, but not the guests, must be able to hear Macbeth talking to the murderer (lines 12 to 32).

a   In pairs or small groups work out where you would position each character for each of the six sections of the scene listed above. Draw six diagrams of the set and write where you would place the appropriate characters on each diagram.

b   Underneath each of the diagrams write down what you, as a director, would want the audience to be thinking and feeling at the end of that section.

c   Using twelve people (taking the roles of Macbeth, Lady Macbeth, Banquo's ghost, the murderer and eight guests) act out the scene using the staging that you drew out in part **a**. Consider:

- How far have you made the scene dynamic? Is there enough movement and tension for the audience to retain their interest?
- Have you positioned the guests correctly for them to hear only what was intended for them?
- Is your staging likely to achieve what you want the audience to be thinking and feeling?

MACBETH AND THE MURDERER

In productions the way that the dialogue between Macbeth and the murderer is staged does a lot to establish the positioning and atmosphere of the rest of the scene.

1 a In groups of four take the roles of Macbeth, the murderer and two guests.

b Act out the scene from line 12 to 32. Begin with the guests seated and Macbeth just about to sit down. The murderer enters. Half way through line 12 Macbeth sees him and sees Banquo's blood on his face. Play the scene as though one of the guests also notices the blood on the murderer's face. Think about how they would react, for example they might try very hard to listen to Macbeth's conversation with the murderer.

c The next time Macbeth sees Banquo's blood it will be on the ghost. Some productions use the murderer as a forerunner to this by having, for example, the murderer and ghost in a similar pose or a similar position on stage. What other ways can you think of, in the staging of the scene, to highlight links between the murderer and the ghost?

d As a director you have several choices in the staging of the conversation between Macbeth and the murderer. They include:

- Macbeth playing the whole scene showing the emotions he talks of ('But now I am cabined, cribbed, confined, bound in') with the guests watching this.
- Macbeth playing the scene without showing this fear, perhaps even laughing or clapping the murderer on the back so that this seems a perfectly normal conversation to the guests. His behaviour is then directly at odds with his speech.

In your groups try different ways of playing the conversation.

e What different effects would each of these choices have on an audience? Do you think, for example, that the audience would be more understanding of Macbeth's behaviour if he is obviously anxious, or if he is able to control his emotions and behaviour?

MACBETH AND THE GHOST

1 a   In pairs or small groups read through lines 40 to 73, and
89 to 107.

   b   How you would stage the two appearances of Banquo's ghost?
Some productions, for example, don't have the ghost appearing on
stage at all, so that only Macbeth 'sees' him. Consider these
questions:

   • If you had Banquo appearing, would you want the actor to be
blood-stained?
   • Would you want the ghost to move naturally, or to be able to
appear and disappear, or to move in an 'inhuman' way?
   • If you did not have Banquo appearing, would you want any
special lighting or sound effects, such as low ghostly noises or
witches' cackles?

2 a   In groups of four take the roles of Macbeth, Lady Macbeth, Ross
and Lennox. Read through the two sections of this scene where the
ghost appears, lines 40 to 73, and 89 to 107.

   b   After each of Macbeth's speeches either Ross or Lennox should
speak their thoughts, to capture the growing sense of horror for the
guests. Read through the scene again adding in their thoughts.

   c   Do the same with Lady Macbeth speaking her thoughts after each
of Macbeth's speeches. At what point (if any) does she realise that
Macbeth is seeing the ghost of Banquo rather than Duncan?

   d   The scene can be extremely effective in production when Lady
Macbeth's fear is as great as that of Macbeth, but while he is afraid
of the vision 'which might appal the devil', her fear is of the
consequences of Macbeth giving away what they have done. What
state of mind would you want Lady Macbeth to be in at the time
the guests leave the banquet?

MACBETH AND LADY MACBETH

The last section of the scene, after the guests have left, reveals shockingly the relationship between Macbeth and Lady Macbeth as it now stands. Although it is only Act 3, it is the last time that we see them together. The banquet has been an important turning point.

1 a Imagine that you are Lady Macbeth at the moment when the guests leave and you are alone with Macbeth. How worried are you that your husband's rule will come to an end because of what he has revealed tonight at the banquet?

b Read through lines 130 to 140 and imagine that you are Lady Macbeth listening to Macbeth's words. Consider:

- How much has Macbeth changed from the man you married?
- How much do you regret actions of yours which have contributed to this change?
- How isolated do you feel when he talks of himself and no longer includes you, for example when he says, 'For mine own good all causes shall give way'?

c Imagine that you are Lady Macbeth. Write a diary entry for the evening of the banquet. As you write, you are trying to work out what happened and why.

ACT 4 SCENE 1: BACK TO THE WITCHES

Each activity in this section leads directly onto the next. However, it is possible to use any of them separately. The focus of the activities is the change in Macbeth since his first meeting with the Witches.

This scene opens with huge expectations from the audience. Macbeth has told us in Act 3 Scene 4 that he will demand to know 'by the worst means, the worst'. Then Hecate, the Witch goddess who calls the Witches to account for helping Macbeth, told us in Act 3 Scene 5 that, after this next meeting, Macbeth will 'spurn fate, scorn death, and bear his hopes 'bove wisdom, grace and fear.' As thunder is heard and the Witches enter we are waiting for these things to happen.

THE WITCHES' SPELL

The first section of this scene (lines 1 to 38) is, in essence, a recipe as the Witches mix up their hellish spell.

1 a In groups of three read lines 4 to 38. It is a very powerful opening to the scene and the chorus alerts us to the 'double' meanings and 'trouble' to come through the rest of the scene. Discuss the effect that this opening of the scene might have on an audience.

   b Pick out a few of the most sickening ingredients, for example:

   WITCH 3   Finger of birth-strangled babe,
                Ditch-delivered by a drab –

   c Consider:

   • What effect might the use of such ingredients have on an audience?
   • In what ways might an audience's feelings towards the Witches have changed since their first appearance in Act 1?

   d In your groups make up a few lines of your own, listing ingredients. Are your ingredients more or less gruesome than those listed in the text?

2   In some productions the ingredients of the spell are scattered around
    the stage as the scene opens. This really is a vision of hell.

    a   Imagine that you are staging the scene in this way. In small groups
        write a description of the stage as the lights go up.

    b   Using a few basic props, for example a doll as the 'babe', set up
        the stage as you have imagined it.

    c   Act out the opening of your scene on your set. Think about what
        atmosphere you want to create. For example, how much do you
        want the Witches to enjoy making the spell?

MACBETH'S CONJURING

When Macbeth goes to meet the Witches, he is very different from the
noble warrior we saw in Act 1. This is a Macbeth who demands to know
the future, whatever it takes.

1   His speech, lines 50 to 61, is a spell matching the power of the spell
    of the Witches.

    a   In small groups construct a freeze-frame for each of the images
        used by Macbeth:

        • Winds unleashed, fighting against the churches
        • Waves swallowing ships
        • Corn and trees blown down and flattened
        • Castles toppled, destroying their keepers
        • Palaces and pyramids collapsing
        • The seeds of all life tumbling towards destruction

    b   Choose one person to be Macbeth. Each of the groups should
        create one of the freeze-frames above. Macbeth should read the
        speech out loud. As he does so, each group should come into
        position in turn so that a hell-like picture of destruction is gradually
        formed.

    c   As each group comes into position, they whisper their line from the
        text, for example, 'Though castles topple', and continue to whisper
        it until the end of the speech. Macbeth then has to build the
        speech in power and intensity in order to be heard.

    d   As a large group discuss the impact that this powerful speech
        would have on an audience. For example, would it change their
        feelings about Macbeth?

APPARITIONS AND PREDICTIONS

1 a In pairs or small groups pick out and list the predictions made by the apparitions. Make a note of Macbeth's response to each one.

  b Discuss the change in Macbeth's attitude to the Witches and the future through this section. Do you think that, by the arrival of the third apparition, Macbeth is spurning fate and bearing his hopes above wisdom as Hecate commanded the Witches to make him do?

2 a Two of the apparitions are children, one bloody and crowned, and one bearing a tree in his hand. In pairs or small groups discuss why children might be chosen to give Macbeth the second and third predictions. Do you think this makes Macbeth more likely to believe the messages that they give?

  b In productions the eight Kings, descendants of Banquo, are also often shown as children. Discuss how you would stage the procession of these eight Kings. For example, would you want the Kings to move naturally and to respond to Macbeth and their surroundings, or perhaps to be unaware of the environment and to move in unison?

MACBETH'S RESOLVE

By the end of the scene Macbeth has resolved to be more bloody and quicker to act upon his murderous thoughts. As soon as he hears that Macduff has escaped to England, he decides to kill Macduff's wife and children.

1 a In groups of three improvise a short scene in which Macbeth hires the murderers.

  b Look back at Act 3 Scene 1 at Macbeth's justification for the murder of Banquo when hiring the killers. Did Macbeth, in your scene, justify these new murders in any way?

ACT 4 SCENE 3: THE ENGLAND SCENE

Each activity in this section leads directly onto the next. However, it is possible to use any of them separately. The focus of the activities is the character of Malcolm and the audience's expectations for the end of the play.

This scene, the only one to take place outside of Scotland, is often shortened or even cut in productions. It is difficult to stage, complex and long. It does, however, shed light on many of the most important themes of the play.

THE ACTION

1 a In pairs take one of the following sections of the scene.

- Lines 1 to 44: Malcolm and Macduff discuss the situation in Scotland and Malcolm expresses his distrust of Macduff.
- Lines 44 to 139: Malcolm pretends to have many deadly vices. When Macduff finally despairs, Malcolm confesses that it was only a test.
- Lines 140 to 159: The Doctor and Malcolm discuss the healing powers of King Edward of England.
- Lines 160 to 192: Ross tells Macduff that his family are well and they talk about the possibility of rebellion happening soon in Scotland.
- Lines 192 to 239: Ross tells Macduff that his family are dead and Malcolm urges Macduff to turn his anger to revenge.

b With your partner read through your section of the scene and then write a short account of what happens in that section. Think of a title for your section.

c With other pairs working on your section, create a freeze-frame to tell the story of your part of the scene. You can use one of your titles as a caption. For example, in the third section, lines 140 to 159, you could show King Edward in the background healing the sick.

THE CHARACTER OF MALCOLM

In order to test Macduff, Malcolm pretends to have all the vices of a tyrant.

1 a In pairs read lines 44 to 99. Make a list of all of these vices, then note down Macduff's response to each.

   b When Macduff despairs for Scotland, Malcolm renounces these vices claiming that he is in fact good and pure and that this is the first time he has spoken falsely. List the good qualities that he then claims he possesses. Does this match with the list of 'king-becoming graces' he had given earlier in lines 91 to 94?

2 Macduff's reaction to these two confessions is key to this scene. In pairs or small groups construct a freeze-frame for each of the following moments:

   • Macduff's despair when he says 'O Scotland! Scotland!' (line 100) Caption the freeze-frame with Macduff's thought.

   • Malcolm asking 'Why are you silent?' (line 137) Caption the freeze-frame with Macduff's thought. Is he relieved or confused? Does he trust Malcolm?

3 How do you see the character of Malcolm? What qualities would you want to bring to the character if you were playing the role? Consider:

   • Is he as 'good' as he professes, do you think? For example, think about how sympathetic he is when Macduff is told that his family are dead.

   • Do you think he has had to become hardened to survive, and to have a chance of deposing Macbeth?

   • If so, do you think this will change the kind of king he will eventually become?

   • How does Malcolm seem to compare with the English King who has the spiritual power to heal the sick?

   • How do you think the way the audience feels about the character of Malcolm might affect the way they feel when Malcolm leads the attack against Macbeth?

THE NEWS FROM SCOTLAND

1 a Read from line 160 to the end of the scene. Why do you think Ross does not give Macduff the dreadful news about his family straight away? Make a list of all the possible reasons.
Example
Ross doesn't want to be blamed for not protecting Macduff's family.

b Which reason would you choose to emphasise in the staging if you were directing the play?

c In pairs improvise the scene between Ross and Macduff, with Ross first lying and then telling the truth.

2 Macduff's pain is so strong that he even brushes aside the comments of Malcolm, his future King, who is urging him to be comforted with thoughts of revenge.

a Make a list of how the audience feel at this moment about:

- Macduff
- Malcolm
- Macbeth

b At the end of this scene, what role do you think the audience expect Malcolm and Macduff to play in the rest of the story?

MACBETH'S DESCENT INTO TYRANNY

The exercises in this character study trace the journey of Macbeth through the play, and in particular the slide from noble warrior to tyrant king. Each activity in this section leads onto the next, but can also be used separately. These activities will work as a revision after close study of the text, or as an introduction.

THE NOBLE WARRIOR

Read through the Captain's account of the battle in Act 1 Scene 2, lines 7 to 42. Use this account to create a short film script of the battle scene with Macbeth as the 'all-action hero' showing his incredible courage. This can be just a list of camera shots or can include speech.

Example

Shot – Macbeth and Macdonwald fighting

Macbeth (calling out): You traitor Macdonwald – you'll die for your sins!

Shot – Macbeth ripping Macdonwald from the stomach to the mouth

THE MURDER OF DUNCAN

a   In pairs read through Macbeth's speech in Act 2 Scene 1, lines 33 to 48, when he sees the imaginary dagger immediately before the murder.

b   Imagine that the dagger is being held and moved by one of the Witches, who is herself invisible. Read the speech through again and while one of you reads the speech, the other should move as the Witch, saying things to tempt Macbeth to murder Duncan.

c   Another interpretation is that the dagger is warning Macbeth of the enormity of the deed he is about to do. Read the speech a third time and while one of you reads the speech the other should speak for the dagger, trying to persuade Macbeth of the horror of murder he intends to commit.

Example

Look, now there is blood on the blade, Duncan's blood, the blood of the King you serve and who has been good to you.

d   With your partner discuss how Macbeth felt when the dagger was tempting him, then how he felt when it was warning him. Consider:

• Why do you think he does not listen to the warning?
• Do you think this is the last moment that he could have turned back?

THE MURDER OF BANQUO

a Read through Macbeth's conversation with Banquo in Act 3 Scene 1, lines 13 to 39, remembering that he has already decided to have Banquo killed. Bear in mind that almost everything Macbeth says in this scene is intended to deceive Banquo.

b Pick out three lines that Macbeth says during the scene. For each one decide what he is really thinking.

Examples

Fail not our feast.	**You won't be there. You'll be dead.**
Goes Fleance with you?	**Say yes! Please say yes, then my assassins can kill Fleance too.**

c Macbeth has said (in Act 1 Scene 7) that he and Lady Macbeth must put on a 'false face'. How easy is this deception for Macbeth, do you think, judging from this scene with Banquo?

THE SIGHT OF BANQUO'S GHOST

a Read through Act 3 Scene 4 or the scene summary on page 114.

b In pairs imagine you were two of the guests at the banquet. You have just watched your King point at a 'bloody' man that no-one else can see, declare that it wasn't he that did 'it', and that there was a time when the dead stayed in their graves. You are now suspicious. Write a short scene in which you are discussing what has happened and what Macbeth's strange comments might mean. Consider these questions:

- Did your character believe Malcolm and Donalbain to be guilty of the murder of King Duncan until this happened?
- Would Macbeth's behaviour at this banquet have changed your mind?

THE SLAUGHTER OF THE CHILDREN

a   Read through Act 4 Scene 2 or the scene summary on page 150. In many ways this is the most violent and shocking scene in the play. Remember that Macbeth already knew that Macduff had fled to England. This means that this wasn't intended as the capture of an enemy, but was revenge and may have been meant to frighten and deter other would-be traitors.

b   In pairs decide exactly what you think happens in the scene. For example, how many children were killed? How were they killed?

c   Now imagine you are one of the murderers reflecting back on the event. Each write an account of what you saw and did.

d   In productions this is often the scene that ensures an audience lose their last remaining sympathy with Macbeth. What do you think the audience would be thinking and feeling at the end of the scene if it was shown as described in your account?

NEW WIDOWS, NEW ORPHANS

In Act 4 Scene 3, lines 4 to 5, Macduff says, 'Each new morn, new widows howl, new orphans cry.' From this and from other comments on how Scotland is suffering we learn that murder at the command of Macbeth is now commonplace and people are very afraid.

a   Choose one of the characters below and read the lines selected for that character.

   • Doctor: Act 5 Scene 1, lines 64 to 72
   • Angus: Act 5 Scene 2, lines 16 to 22

b   Think about what it would be like to live as that character in Macbeth's Scotland. Write a short conversation in which you are telling a friend who has been out of the country for some time what it has been like.

TYRANNY OR MADNESS?

It is usually Lady Macbeth who is associated with madness, but Macbeth has shown signs of a disturbed mind all the way through the play, for example seeing imaginary daggers, and hearing voices in his mind. Certainly Macbeth changes greatly through the play. He goes from a man who 'starts' at every noise just after the killing of Duncan to a man who, in some productions, seems entirely disconnected from his emotions by the end of the play.

a Read aloud the following speech from Act 5 Scene 5:

> **MACBETH**   I have almost forgot the taste of fears.
> The time has been, my senses would have cooled
> To hear a night-shriek; and my fell of hair
> Would, at a dismal treatise, rouse and stir,
> As life were in 't. I have supped full with horrors:
> Direness, familiar to my slaughterous thoughts,
> Cannot once start me.

b In pairs decide which of you is going to be a prosecution lawyer and which of you is going to be a defence lawyer at the trial of Macbeth. The prosecution lawyer should argue that Macbeth was a murderous tyrant. The defence lawyer should argue that he was not responsible for his own actions, either because of madness or because the Witches caused him to be possessed by the devil. For example, being possessed might have made him more vulnerable to the taunts of Lady Macbeth.

c Go through the play and gather your evidence. For example, if you were defending Macbeth, you might use the fact that he is 'rapt' (in a trance), after hearing the Witches' prophecies, as a clear indication that he is under their spell.

d Each of you should prepare a speech which summarises your arguments.

e Both lawyers should read their speeches, prosecution followed by defence. Then each lawyer should challenge the other's arguments.